CREATION
or
EVOLUTION?

Also by Michael Ebifegha

Farewell to Darwinian Evolution
The Darwinian Delusion
4th Origin: Refuting the Myth of Evolutionism
and Exposing the Folly of Clergy Letters
Origin: Satan's Shadow in Religion

CREATION or EVOLUTION?

Origin of Species in Light of Science's
Limitations and Historical Records

Michael Ebifegha

Creation or Evolution?

Copyright © 2022 by Michael Ebifegha. All rights reserved.

No part of this publication may be reproduced, stored in a retrieval system or transmitted in any way by any means, electronic, mechanical, photocopy, recording or otherwise without the prior permission of the author except as provided by USA copyright law.

The opinions expressed by the author are not necessarily those of URLink Print and Media.

1603 Capitol Ave., Suite 310 Cheyenne, Wyoming USA 82001
1-888-980-6523 | admin@urlinkpublishing.com

URLink Print and Media is committed to excellence in the publishing industry.

Book design copyright © 2022 by URLink Print and Media. All rights reserved.

Published in the United States of America
Library of Congress Control Number: 2022907923
ISBN 978-1-68486-173-6 (Paperback)
ISBN 978-1-68486-174-3 (Hardback)
ISBN 978-1-68486-175-0 (Digital)
21.04.22

To the
↓
Sempiternal
↓
Immutable
↓
Immaterial
↓
Omnipotent
↓
Omnipresent
↓
Omniscient
↓
GOD

CONTENTS

Welcome 9
Preface 13
Introduction 19
Chapter 1   Constraints In Science 31
Chapter 2   Creationism And Evolutionism Compared 55
Chapter 3   The Irrelevance Of The Earth's Age To
              The Creationist/Evolutionist Controversy 70
Chapter 4   The Origin Of Life And Species Limitations 76
Chapter 5   The Natural Selection Limitation 85
Chapter 6   Similarity/Dissimilarity Limitations 90
Chapter 7   The Natural History Limitation 102
Chapter 8   Writing Off Darwinism 112
Chapter 9   The Myth Of The Grand Design By Chaos 129
Chapter 10 The Historical Record Of God's Patent
              And Seal On Creation 142
Conclusion 167
Appendix 175
Acknowledgments 177
References/Notes 179
Index 203

WELCOME

Science is not the avenue of truth in unfolding mysteries, such as when, where, and how a person was born. To establish the truth, scientists, just like everybody else, would require a detailed record of the person's birth or an eyewitness of an event. If none is available, various just-so answers can be established through the collection of circumstantial evidence, improvable theories, and expert opinion. These answers are outside the limits of true science; hence, it comes down to an issue of choices and endless debates—so too is the situation concerning the birth of the universe and its various life-forms. We are confronted with choices: creation or evolution. Sharing their experience in this battle for truth, evolutionists Jerry Fodor and Massimo Piattelli-Palmarini in *What Darwin Got Wrong*[1] wrote:

> This is not a book about God; nor about intelligent design; nor about creationism. Neither of us is into any of those. We thought we'd best make that clear from the outset, because our main contention in what follows will be that there is something wrong—quite possibly fatally wrong— with the theory of natural selection; and we are aware that, even among those who are not quite sure what it is, allegiance to Darwinism has become a litmus for deciding who does, and

---

[1] Jerry Fodor and Massimo Piattelli-Palmarini, *What Darwin Got Wrong* (New York: Farrar, Straus, and Giroux, 2010), pp. xiii, xx.

who does not, hold a "properly scientific" world view. "You must choose between faith in God and faith in Darwin; and if you want to be a secular humanist, you'd better choose the latter." So we're told.

We doubt that those options are exhaustive. But we do want, ever so much, to be secular humanists. In fact, we both claim to be outright, card-carrying, signed-up, dyed-in-the-wool, no-holds-barred atheists.

We close these prefatory comments with a brief homily: we've been told by more than one of our colleagues that, even if Darwin was substantially wrong to claim that natural selection is the mechanism of evolution, nonetheless we shouldn't say so. Not, anyhow, in public. To do that is, however inadvertently, to align oneself with the Forces of Darkness, whose goal it is to bring Science into disrepute. Well, we don't agree. We think the way to discomfort the Forces of Darkness is to follow the arguments wherever they may lead, spreading such light as one can in the course of doing so. What makes the Forces of Darkness dark is that they aren't willing to do that. What makes Science scientific is that it is.

After over a century of analyzing the birth of the universe and its various life-forms, the choice between creation and evolution has narrowed to a belief in what God revealed in speech before an assembly of Israelites in the Sinai Desert or what Charles Darwin, as a scientist, theorized to be the truth. Because a claim of ownership is a historic and civil affair, and because the subject of origin is outside the purview of science, the choice is not between religion and science but between a creator's narrative and a creature's opinion. The circumstantial evidence in the world, not individual preference, should be the veridical guide. The reader is welcome to explore the various ideas and follow the arguments, wherever these may lead.

Jerry Fodor is a professor of philosophy and cognitive science at Rutgers University. Massimo Piattelli-Palmarini is a biophysicist, molecular biologist, and professor of cognitive science at the University of Arizona.

PREFACE

Being an instructor in the field of science at both the secondary and postsecondary levels has been a rewarding experience. With a certificate in religious education from the Toronto Catholic District School Board, I have maintained a keen interest in the physical world that is accessible to science. In the teaching profession, one meets people from all walks of life with different backgrounds and beliefs. Some believe in Mother Nature, others only in science, and still others in both science and religion. If science is to credibly address issues that are of interest to organized religion, it must avoid schismatic divisions. How can science relate harmoniously to religion without scientists having to align themselves as creationists or evolutionists? The unity of the scientific establishment is only possible when science remains within its disciplinary limitations and draws from, rather than competes with, other sources of truth that are outside its limitations.

Science has contributed immensely to a better life. Computers have become an essential part of our everyday lives. Cell phones enable us to communicate instantaneously across the globe. Physicians can cure diseases and injuries that would have been fatal just a few decades ago. Microwaves allow us to heat or reheat our meals in a matter of seconds. Thanks to science we can now even travel into the stratosphere.

But all of the above scientific achievements depend on one thing: the testability and repeatability of phenomena. Accordingly, while studies of the structure, composition, and dynamics of DNA fall within the purview of science, studies of the *origin* of DNA do not, because this event is not testable and repeatable. We thus cannot judge studies relating to origins by the same standard as that of everyday experience. Accordingly, the study of origins can be classified as pseudoscience, which denotes a combination of scientific ideas and preferred beliefs about the unknowable past that are beyond scientific validation or falsification. It is rather demeaning that, whenever many in the field of origins science publicize their research, they present their findings as having the same degree of credibility and accuracy as those of scientists engaged in studies relating to our everyday use of science in our homes or hospitals. And whenever the credibility of their deductions is challenged, they respond by listing the history of achievements in our everyday life, as the evidence to believe their stories. Masking the subjective presuppositions of their paradigm, evolutionists present their dead-end conclusions as scientific facts.

Science is unaffected by the beginning of things, so it should not matter to science whether the world was created or evolved. For this reason, no scientific discovery comes stamped with the label of either creationism or evolutionism. However, it matters to modern scientists because the former supports theism, whereas the latter endorses materialism. The debate has deteriorated to the extent that judges have to rule on what constitutes science versus pseudoscience. The distinction between the two rests squarely on our ability to recognize the limitations of science.

On the one hand, organisms have a material dimension that science can describe; on the other hand, they possess an immaterial dimension (i.e., soul or spirit) that science cannot observe. What this means is that scientific studies of life's origins are based exclusively on material things such as DNA and fossils. Consequently, they are inadequate foundations for establishing the truth concerning life's provenance. Given these circumstances, it is impossible to develop any reliable scientific theory that explains the origins or genealogies of living things.

In their recent book titled *The Grand Design*, Stephen Hawking and Leonard Mlodinow posit that scientists can now address questions traditionally reserved for philosophers because philosophy is now allegedly dead.[1] In the field of life's origins, scientists, therefore, make all sorts of assumptions such as "punctuated equilibrium" and the "spontaneous generation of life" that are not testable but are widely accepted because they eliminate the need for intelligent agency. Scientists as philosophers are rank amateurs. According to Nobel laureate Ernst Boris Chain, "Scientists are often just as prejudiced in their theories and emotionally involved in the implications of their work as are other nonscientific members of society, and are unreliable in their predictions and interpretations."[2] Honest evolutionists do not deny that some of their conclusions are ridiculous. For instance, in 1977 Stephen Jay Gould and his colleagues published an article declaring that "Paleontologists (and evolutionary biologists in general) are famous for their facility in devising plausible stories, but they often forget that plausible stories need not be true."[3] Scientists in the field of life's origins come up with conflicting conclusions because the evidence they present as scientific facts cannot be tested or replicated.

Not all scientists accept such philosophical assumptions as the spontaneous generation of life. This is bad science because it is not based on empirical evidence. Hence, the scientific establishment splits into creationists and evolutionists. Evolutionists, many of whom are atheists, stick to the hypothesis of abiogenesis, which parallels the notion of resurrection from dead matter. Creationists, on the other hand, endorse the scientific law of biogenesis, which stipulates that life can derive only from preexisting life. Which camp of scientists should we believe?

The living world is where we encounter the reality of a complete organism endowed with both material and immaterial dimensions.

How can the Darwinian model of evolution be scientific fact when there is zero evidence of transitional stages in the living world? Darwin's theory of evolution is not based on laws or experiments; it is based on historical assumptions, such as, common descent of all species, gradualism, competition, and natural selection. It is a theory on diversity and not on origin of species. At the empirical level, no species of bacteria has been formed gradually through competition (a struggle in which organisms best suited to an environment survive and reproduce while others perish) as the Darwinian paradigm predicts; on the contrary, new species of bacteria are instead produced rapidly through collaboration.[4] The empirical evidence therefore refutes the Neo-Darwinian paradigm of evolution. This suggests that natural selection is not the engine or primary mechanism of evolution. The rapid formation of new species through collaboration, rather, resonates with the biblical creation narratives.

"Why," we might ask, "is the scientific worldview limited to evolution as a natural process and not to both evolution and creation as natural processes at the micro level?" By restricting itself to the paradigmatic model of evolutionism, the scientific community effectively blinds itself to alternative and equally compelling models of life's aboriginal source.

The creationist worldview was in existence before Darwin reinforced the evolutionist worldview in his revolutionary book *The Origin of Species* (1859). The scientific establishment since then has written off creationism as falling outside science because the events cannot be tested and the mechanism is unknowable. However, after a century and a half of extensive research on biological evolution, not even one bacterium has been transformed by either artificial or natural selection, confirming that evolution also lies outside the limitations of science as an untestable and unrepeatable event. Hence, when it comes to the origin of species, evolution is not a scientific fact but only an unknowable mechanism. The time has now come to write off an evolutionist perspective.

This book is unique from other books on creationism and evolutionism because it examines these worldviews solely within the limits of science. Because it deals with the realities of our physical world, the book will be a valuable guide for those who seek the truth and are not afraid to follow the scientific evidence wherever it leads.

INTRODUCTION

We find it most inappropriate that some well-meaning scientists have given the impression that there can only be one scientific view concerning origins. By doing so they are going way beyond the limits of empirical science which has to recognize, at the very least, severe limitations concerning origins. No one has proved experimentally the idea that large variations can emerge from simpler life forms in an unbroken ascendancy to man. A large body of scientific evidence in biology, geology, and chemistry, as well as the fundamentals of information theory, strongly suggest that evolution is not the best scientific model to fit the data that we observe.[1]

—Andy McIntosh DSc, Edgar Andrews PhD, DSc, et al.

Evolutionary biology is essentially a collection of folktales told by leading modern biologists. Titles like *The Selfish Gene*, *The Blind Watchmaker*, *River Out of Eden*, *Climbing Mount Improbable*, *Unweaving the Rainbow*, and *The Ancestor's Tale* fit neatly in the library of evolutionary tales.[2]

—Michael Ebifegha

Our five senses—hearing, sight, touch, smell, and taste—define our ability to study the world through observation and measurement; hence, our senses limit science to the material realm. In the study of living systems, however, we encounter both the material (e.g., the brain) and the immaterial (e.g., the mind). With the fossils of chimpanzees and humans, for instance, scientists deal with only the material components, so they can link similarities in brain structure and DNA to a supposedly common ancestry, triggering the search for missing links in biological evolution by natural selection. However, the absence of transitional stages in the Cambrian record of fossils militates against the theory of evolution by natural selection as the likely mechanism. In the living world, when scientists examine chimpanzees and humans, marked dissimilarities in their immaterial nature outweigh similarities in their material realm. This fact, together with the absence of transitional species, disqualifies evolution by natural selection as an exclusive mechanism. Since a unifying theory of living systems must address both material and immaterial aspects, Darwinistic science falls short as an explanatory construct.

Science is unique in its attempt to explain the phenomenal world in terms of natural processes and laws. The existence of such laws is evidence that nature itself is caused, sustained, and guided. Creation and evolution are unique processes that shape and modify the physical world. DNA replication, cell division, and protein production are all natural processes of creation. Modifications in the creative process may result in horizontal changes that become the raw products for evolution as a secondary process. To be true, therefore, a comprehensive theory of species' origins must integrate the processes of both creation and evolution. This deduction further confirms the fact that there can be no unifying theory based exclusively on evolution. The term "creation" as designating a natural process is not controversial in other fields of science except evolutionary biology, where it invariably implies a creator.

In this field, the scientific establishment elaborates evolution as a scientific fact and deems creation a religious myth. Evolutionary biology is a historical science: the synonyms for evolution (i.e., growth, change, development, progression, advancement) are, scientifically speaking, indistinguishable from the synonyms of creation (i.e., design, construction, establishment, formation). To distance creation from evolution, modern scientists generally define evolution as "change through time." However, change through time could be the direct consequence of either creation or evolution or neither. For instance, the aging process is change through time in that organisms metamorphose under the influence of drugs, genetic mutation, environmental factors, and climate change. Therefore, not all change through time can be attributed exclusively to the process of evolution.

The only change through time that is unique to evolutionary biology is the Darwinian claim that all life emerged from a single origin (bacteria-to-human transitions) under the instrumentality of chance and natural selection. For purposes of clarification, this discourse refers to this category as "Darwinian change through time." Thus, whereas "change through time" or "descent with modification" describes the "bacteria-to-bacteria" or "finch-to-finch" modifications that are consistent with either creationist or evolutionist worldviews, "Darwinian change through time" or "descent with transformation" describes "bacteria-to-human" transitions, a concept that is limited to the evolutionist worldview. For example, we can witness and produce different breeds of dog or cat (descent with modification), but we can neither discover in the fossil record nor produce in the living world organisms that are half dog and half cat or something else (descent with transformation). (I have ruled out the platypus because it has its own unique characteristics and for over 100 million years in the evolutionary time-scale there is only evidence of platypus-to-platypus modifications.) The appeal to millions of years for such transitions to materialize is an "evolutionism of the gaps," but such a time span is outside the practical limits of scientific investigation and falsification.

While it is not possible to develop a general theory of evolution as Jerry Fodor and Massimo Piattelli-Palmarini affirm,[3] we cannot abandon creationist and evolutionist worldviews entirely as they are now part and parcel of our belief systems. On the one hand, creationism and evolutionism are beliefs of the past that scientists cannot prove, observe, or reproduce; on the other hand, both paradigms examine the same scientific evidence but offer different interpretations and conclusions. The scientific establishment and the media are simply wrong when they present creationism as a religious enterprise and evolutionism as a scientific paradigm. The goal of this book is to examine both models in light of science's limitations. My discussions will center on the evolutionist worldview because it is the only one the scientific establishment acknowledges as scientific fact. The creationist model incorporates some degree of changes within species, which biologists refer to as microevolution—the evidential form of descent with modification. Creationism is therefore more accommodating than evolutionism.

Fodor and Piattelli-Palmarini posit that "biologists have changed Neo-Darwinism in many ways; the point now is to subvert it."[4] However, not just the insufficiency of the Darwinian paradigm is the issue at stake; instead, it is the inability of science as a body of knowledge to address the subject of origins. The main thesis of this discourse is that authentic analysis of the origins of species demands knowledge of both the material and immaterial realms, including apodictic knowledge of the origin of life. The desired information is outside the domain of empirical science. The correct answer to the origins of species lies, instead, within the domain of history.

Chapter 1 examines the constraints of science as an explanatory framework for the origin of species. Science, the study of the physical universe, is at its best when its conclusions are limited to events or processes manifest within the empirical realm. Some disciples of scientism, presumably in order to compete with religious doctrines, evidently believe that they can blend the physical and metaphysical realms under the guise of materialism. When science exceeds its boundaries, truth is compromised. Mingling belief with science robs the latter of its objective impartiality. My first chapter, therefore, challenges scientists who compromise their discipline's integrity in order to salvage Darwinism, a pseudoscientific concept.

Chapter 2 compares our contemporary world to a hypothetical world exclusively under the influence of evolutionary processes and agency. If chance is instrumental in shaping the universe, why does it obey natural laws that are antithetical to chance? If nonintelligence is behind the marvelous designs we observe, why should we need intelligence to investigate the evidence correctly? Why should the age of the universe or the earth determine whether we are the products of creation or evolution?

Chapter 3 considers the irrelevance of the earth's age to the creationist/evolutionist controversy. In *The Darwinian Delusion: The Scientific Myth of Evolutionism*, I pointed out the triviality of this debate concerning the earth's age.[5] Concern with the earth's age tells us nothing about its inhabitants and supports neither creationism nor evolutionism. Scientists have used the argument, however, to validate evolutionism and mythicize creationism. This book's third chapter thus presents an unbiased clarification of the controversy.

The origin of fossils is radically different from the origin of species. If our interest is in the origin of fossils, then, because fossils are lifeless, knowledge of the origin of life is not essential. Species, however, have life; and just as we cannot separate the origin of our brains from the origin of our minds, scientists cannot isolate the origin of species from the origin of life. Because scientists presently do not know how life originated, they cannot correctly explain the origin of species.

Chapter 4 stresses the fact that knowledge of the intersection between the origin of life (independent component) and the origin of species (dependent component) is required to establish the latter. This book argues that the Darwinian tree of life, which provides a genealogy of the origin of species, is wrong without a prior knowledge of the origin of life. Without correct knowledge of how life originated, the theory of the origin of species that Neo-Darwinists present as scientific fact is unfit for inclusion in any science curriculum that eschews the teaching of metaphysical persuasions. Because the National Academy of Sciences and Institute of Medicine affirms "biological evolution accounts for events that are also central concerns of religion,"[6] continued teaching of the Darwinian paradigm of evolution would suggest that the state and the media are deliberately endorsing the teaching of religious tenets in science classes. If the origin of life is unknowable through science, scientists must accept their limitations and refrain from teaching secular doctrines as scientific facts.

Leading evolutionists such as Richard Dawkins in *The God Delusion* (2006), ignoring the limits of science, posit that the mindless process of natural selection is behind the sophistication and diversity of species. Fortunately Dawkins' colleagues, evolutionists Fodor and Piattelli-Palmarini, who share his atheism, argue in *What Darwin Got Wrong* that the theory of natural selection is irredeemably wrong. They reject Darwin's theory not on religious grounds but rather on the strength of good science spanning molecular, behavioral, cognitive, and evolutionary-developmental biology. I have previously addressed natural selection in *The Darwinian Delusion*.[7] Chapter 5 of the present book augments that discussion in the light of Fodor and Piattelli-Palmarini's brilliant work.

The designer of DNA as a blueprint for life had two choices in generating diversity with both similarity and dissimilarity. The first option was to generate the desired diversity within a short duration of time. With wisdom and understanding the designer would generate multiple blueprints with varying degrees of complexity characterizing each basic kind, with mechanisms for reproduction and an allowance for variation within the basic kinds. Consider, for instance, how computers have progressed from Microsoft Windows 1, 2, 3.0, NT, 95, 98, 2000, XP, to VISTA. The designer of DNA could generate diversity in intervals of, say, minutes, hours, or days. The second option was for the designer to provide the first prototype of a blueprint and then use another less efficient instrumentality to generate diversity. Depending on the nature of the instrumentality, this would require many years to produce diversity. Option 1 parallels the creationist worldview in Genesis with allowance for variation within the organisms' boundaries (e.g., farmyard breeding or microevolution). Option 2 parallels the evolutionist worldview that advocates bacteria-to-human evolution (macroevolution). Both options are equally probable statistically; hence, similarity arguments do not favour any particular worldview. A majority of scientists, however, choose the evolutionist worldview because (1) it justifies an old earth, and (2) it removes the direct role of a creator in the diversity of species. Chapter 6 addresses science's limitations in deploying similarity/dissimilarity arguments in the debate about creationism versus evolutionism.

Chapter 7 focuses on the lack of historical evidence to justify an evolutionary worldview. Evidence of transitional stages is missing both in the living world and in the "Cambrian explosions" at Burgess Shale in the Canadian Rockies and at the Chengjiang site in China.[8] It is only proper at this point that we demand hard evidence of transitional stages. To wait millions of years for it to appear is simply a scientism of the gaps. This book contends that evolution as a natural process, just like creation, is a fact, but that Darwinian brand of evolution or change over time is a myth.

For scientific reasons, *New Scientist* of January 24–30, 2009, insists that "Darwin was Wrong" (www.NewScientist.com) and that it is time to cut down the tree of life. Fodor and Piattelli-Palmarini explain the major problem in their book *What Darwin Got Wrong* and demand that the tree needs to be cut at its roots because it is fatally flawed and apparently misleading research studies in other fields far removed from biology.[9] Before the above publications, W. Ford Doolittle, in the February 2000 issue of the *Scientific American* published the groundbreaking article, "Uprooting the Tree of Life."[10] Mary H. Schweitzer's article, "Blood from Stone"[11] in the December 2010 issue of the *Scientific American*, challenges the validity of evolutionary predictions. Chapter 8 details why Darwinism must be written off.

One of science's great achievements in the past decade is the Large Hadron Collider (LHC). The European Organization for Nuclear Research built this magnificent system in collaboration with over 10,000 scientists and engineers from 100 countries, as well as hundreds of universities and laboratories, at a cost of $9 billion.[12,13] The overall purpose of LHC is to understand the Big Bang. The LHC project involved several phases of serious thinking, planning, and constructing. It is therefore mind-boggling for scientists to posit that what took them years of focused effort to implement happened accidentally and spontaneously during the world's creation.

Analogically, a grand design without a designer is like the LHC installation without scientists and engineers. Chapter 9 therefore refutes Stephen Hawking and Leonard Mlodinow's recent assertion that "It is not necessary to invoke God to light the blue touch paper and set the universe going."[14]

With Darwinism dead and buried and with the necessity of a designer in the grand design, what does the future hold for biological evolution? Fodor and Piattelli-Palmarini posit that "The story about the evolution of phenotypes belongs to natural history and not to biology."[15] Accordingly, biological evolution should be confined to the limits achieved in artificial selection. What then becomes of the origins question? The subject lies outside the domain of natural history; no one observed events at the beginning of life. Accordingly, the truth about origins can come only from historical revelation. Science's limitations rule out the role of biology, and human limitations disqualify natural history as a mode of investigation in our search for answers about the origin of species.

We must look beyond ourselves for the truth concerning origins. Honest answers must begin with honest questions that consider all possibilities—creation and/or evolution. Integrity demands that preference must not be the rule. The fact that a particular mechanism may not be understandable does not preclude its viability. Apparently, however, the scientific establishment prefers evolution and rejects creation not because it understands the mechanism behind either as the designing instrumentality but simply because creation presupposes a creator.

Once we rule out preferences, the next step is to examine all logical scenarios. The only appropriate recourse now is to direct the same effort expended on the evolutionary scenario toward analyzing the creation scenario. This effort would begin by brainstorming all the things that characterize an invention such as a claim, seal, or patent of ownership. In the event that there are claims, the unprejudiced scientist would proceed to investigate their credibility. It is in this spirit that physicist Colin J. Humphreys reports in *The Miracles of Exodus* how for over two decades he used science to establish the accuracy of the Exodus story in the Old Testament.[16] Hawking and Mlodinow in *The Grand Design* discussed at length how creation myths attempt to answer the questions they address in their book: Why is there a universe, and why is the universe the way it is? They made special reference to the Mayan legend the Maker, and the great god Bumba, who, according to the Boshongo people of central African, out of pain vomited the sun, moon, stars, and then some animals: the leopard, the crocodile, the turtle, and finally man.[17] The creation myth of the Boshongo people is in many ways similar to the spontaneous creation myth that Hawking and Mlodinow present in *The Grand Design*. In particular, the role of the god Bumba is accomplished by the law of gravity in Hawking and Mlodinow's story on how the universe came into existence. In their account of God's creation, Hawking and Mlodinow simply wrote, "According to the Old Testament, God created Adam and Eve only six days into creation."[18] These are all stories or theories of creation; what is required is an evidence of the creator's claim of ownership before an audience. In this regard John Rennie, the chief editor of *Scientific American* (2002) promised "If super intelligent aliens appeared and claimed credit for creating life on earth (or even particular species), the purely evolutionary explanation would be cast in doubt. But no one has yet produced such evidence."[19] This makes sense.

Chapter 10 discusses God's personal claim before an audience of Jews around 1445 BC to have created the world. Many within and outside the scientific establishment may find it difficult to credit a claim they deem religious in nature. In fact, however, God's claim is an historical event reported in secular literature (see, for example, books on Jewish history by historians such as Flavius Josephus).[20]

Humans cannot understand how God could have created the universe in six days as claimed before an audience of ancient Israelites. Scientists, therefore, cannot rule on the accuracy of the claim. It is outside the limits of science to disprove the existence of a supernatural deity; it similarly is outside the limits of science to discredit any such supernatural claims. No one knows empirically what existed before life or what comes after it. Try as we may, some secrets belong only to God; others God shares through either direct revelation or science. In the words of distinguished physicist H. S. Lipson, "The Designer must know infinitely more science than we shall ever know."[21] Lipson, a Fellow of the Royal Society, is simply being honest.

With God, who is immaterial, claiming credit for having created the world, the immaterial realm of living things that is outside science's limit is accounted for. In the material realm God restricts life forms to produce or diversify according to their kind. Microevolutionary science validates God's restrictions in the laboratory as viruses only evolve to new variants or strains; they do not evolve across their boundary. Hence, God's claim together with the scientific evidence provides the full account for the origin and diversity of species. This book, therefore, proposes *creation-evolution unison* as opposed to a *creation-evolution controversy* in order to account for the immaterial and material attributes of our universe. In the *creation-evolution unison* no scientist is a creationist or evolutionist; a scientist is simply a scientist.

CHAPTER 1

CONSTRAINTS IN SCIENCE

> Science knows about objective reality, the mask of matter that our five senses detect. But the mind goes beyond the five senses. And what lies beyond the boundary of the five senses holds enormous mysteries, and it does Dawkins no good to lump the two worlds of inner and outer together.[1]
>
> —Deepak Chopra

> The appearance of similar abilities in distantly related species, but not necessarily in closely related ones, illustrates that cognitive traits cannot be neatly arranged on an evolutionary scale of relatedness.[2]
>
> —Johan J. Bolhuis and Clive D. L. Wynne

I was drawn to Kat McGowan's article titled "Uncovered: How a Brain Creates a Mind"[3] that was published in the special thirty-year-anniversary issue of *Discover* magazine. I glanced through the article, but there was not much information to justify the title. The nature of the relationship between the brain (matter) and mind (nonmatter) could lead to different philosophical conclusions, so my curiosity led me to search for the web definition of terms in the field of philosophy. We will examine some of these definitions and their implications.

MATERIALISM VERSUS DUALISM

We have the choice to believe in either physical reality only (materialism) or in physical reality and spiritual reality (dualism). There are several definitions/designations of materialism and dualism on the Web, but we will stick to the ones that relate to the thesis of this book. Materialism is the philosophical belief that matter is all there is, and all phenomena (including consciousness, thought, feeling, mind, and will) are the result of material interaction.[4] In contrast to materialism, dualism is the philosophical belief that reality is essentially divided into two basic ontological categories such as mental (mind) and physical (brain) stuff, spirit (soul) and matter (body), good and evil, male and female, creator and created.[5]

Religion addresses dualism; for instance, in Genesis 1:2, there is reference to the spirit of God and matter (water, earth) and many references to soul and body elsewhere in the Bible. Many accomplished scientists believe in dualism. Expressing his belief in spiritual reality, Albert Einstein said:

> Everyone who is seriously engaged in the pursuit of science becomes convinced that the laws of nature manifest the existence of a spirit vastly superior to that of men, and one in the face of which we with our modest powers must feel humble.[6]

> My religion consists of a humble admiration of the illimitable superior spirit who reveals himself in the slight details we are able to perceive with our frail and feeble minds. That deeply emotional conviction of the presence of a superior reasoning power, which is revealed in the incomprehensible universe, forms my idea of God.[7]

While religion teaches dualism, our five senses, however, limit the scope of science to the material realm; hence, knowledge of the immaterial or spiritual realm is beyond its legitimate purview. Accordingly, many scientists, especially atheist, stick to materialism only. For instance, Richard Lewontin believes that materialism is absolute and no divine foot must be allowed in the door.[8] Nature limits science, but has nature imposed similar limitations on human experience and perception of the world?

Science is only one unique way of searching for truth. The mere fact that, due to its disciplinary limitations, science cannot detect an immaterial or spiritual world does not preclude the possibility of its existence. For example, science's inability to explain the dynamics of love does not mean that love does not exist. The concept of a spiritual world is a natural experience. According to Paul Bloom of Yale University, "[R]eligion is an inescapable artifact of the wiring in our brain, and all humans possess the brain circuitry … that never goes away."[9] Olivera Petrovich of Oxford University posits that "[E]ven adults who describe themselves as atheists and agnostics are prone to supernatural thinking."[10] The point is that no human being is devoid of a religiously oriented consciousness. We should, however, respect the fact that people have different levels of religious affiliation, but also accept the fact that because of natural constraints science can only provide partial truth about our universe. However, while spirit (soul) and matter (body) dualism may be excused on the grounds that is not a uniform or regular human experience, the mind and matter (brain) dualism is a common human experience and hence cannot be ignored. The article "Uncovered: How a Brain Creates a Mind" in Discover is accordingly listed as one of the twelve breakthroughs that transformed the world.

COMMONSENSE DUALISM

According to Bloom, matter and mind are autonomous systems, "leaving us with two viewpoints on the world: one that deals with minds, and one that handles physical aspects of the world."[11] If Kat McGowan is right and a brain (matter) creates a mind, then matter and mind are not autonomous systems leaving us with only one viewpoint of the world. Who is right?

Take, for instance, if *good* creates *bad*, then the *good* and *bad* dualism becomes nonfunctional, so if the natural processes of the brain create the mind, the mind and brain dualism is compromised and we expect radical changes in the functioning of the mind. For instance, because the mind will now depend on the brain, the only way we can change our minds is when the activities in the brain change. In contrast, a mind independent of the brain can change at will, and this is consistent with our experience. A mind that depends on the brain for its creation will also be subject to the laws of matter and may function in a mechanical fashion, similar to a computer that is run by a program; emotions, desires, beliefs, and free choice may cease to exist.[12]

Because science does not understand how the mind works, I searched the Scriptures for information on brain and mind. Nothing was on brain, but there were several references to the human mind. The Scriptures posit that God searches human minds (Ps. 7:9) and will put his law in their minds (Jer. 31:33). These verses, therefore, suggest that human minds are reservoirs of nonmaterial information similar to a computer software package. Because the software is independent of the central processing unit, the mind should be independent of the brain. Mapping consciousness is not the same thing as a brain creating a mind; it likely means a brain (CPU) detecting or processing a mind (software). Accordingly, this discourse will stick to Bloom's assertion that mind and body are autonomous systems.

EVOLUTION AND THE MIND

The focus of evolutionary biology is on species and their development through the ages. To be credible, any scientific theory pertaining to the origin of living things in the universe must consider both their material and immaterial aspects.

The fact that matter and mind are distinct, which Bloom calls "common-sense dualism,"[13] limits the validity of theories such as Charles Darwin's based on limited circumstantial evidence in the material realm, especially as concerns the disputed origin of species based on homologous physical traits. Species, however, are dissimilar in their immaterial nature. Darwin himself alludes to this fact in the following declaration: "There can be no doubt that the difference between the mind of the lowest man and that of the highest animal is immense."[14] He continues, "The difference would, no doubt, still remain immense, even if one of the higher apes had been improved or civilized as much as a dog has been in comparison with its parent form, the wolf or jackal."[15] Darwin further affirms, "The difference in mental power between the highest ape and the lowest savage is immense.[16] And also the difference in mental power between an ant and a coccus is immense."[17] Because of the remarkable differences in the immaterial realm, Darwin was concerned that the conclusion derived from the material realm could be wrong; he wrote:

> [M]an bears in his bodily structure clear traces of his descent from some lower form; but it may be urged that, as man differs so greatly in his mental power from all other animals, there must be some error in this conclusion.[18]

Darwin was fully aware of the immense limitation his theory suffered, but his will to put religion aside prevailed over reason. When it comes to the subject of life's origins, no person thus can claim to be neutral; scholars will always have a philosophical preference. The National Academy of Sciences and Institute of Medicine (NASIM), in its 2008 booklet titled *Science, Evolution, and Creationism*, affirms the following: "Because biological evolution accounts for events that are also central concerns of religion—including the origins of biological diversity and especially the origins of humans—evolution has been a contentious idea within society since it was first articulated by Charles Darwin and Alfred Russell Wallace in 1858."[19] Darwin and Wallace came up with similar scientific information on evolution and natural selection but differed in their philosophical inferences. Darwin's views were limited to the material realm, but Wallace focused on both the material and immaterial realms and concluded that natural selection was not an all-sufficient cause of man's evolution.

For over a century, scientific evidence has consistently pointed to an immaterial and creative intelligence in line with Wallace's unpopular views. Wallace's offense was his opinion that "natural selection was not an all-sufficient cause of the evolution of man—particularly as regards the higher human faculties (moral, artistic, and mathematical abilities, etc.)."[20] The bad news for the scientific establishment is mounting evidence against natural selection as a designing instrumentality for the origins of life. Darwin's views on mind are now widely challenged by some biologists. Johan J. Bolhuis and Clive D. L. Wynne in their essay "Can Evolution Explain How Minds Work?" wrote:

> Darwin's theory of evolution by natural selection is broadly accepted among biologists, but its implications for the study of cognition are far from clear. ... In *The Descent of Man*, Darwin proposed that there is "no fundamental difference between man and the higher mammals in their mental faculties" on the basis of his belief that all living species were descended from a common ancestor ... [F]indings have cast doubt on the straightforward application of Darwinism to cognition. Some have even called Darwin's

idea of continuity of mind a mistake. ... Another major stumbling block is that it is extremely difficult, if not impossible, to identify the factors that originally drove the emergence of contemporary animal and human traits. ... For comparative psychology to progress, we must study animal and human minds empirically, without naïve evolutionary presuppositions.[21]

Marc Hauser is a Professor of Psychology and Evolutionary Biology, and co-director of the Mind, Brain, and Behaviour Program at Harvard University. Hauser in his essay "Origin of the Mind" wrote:

> Before Charles Darwin argued in his 1871 book *The Descent of Man* that the difference between human and nonhuman minds is "one of degree and not of kind." Scholars have long upheld that view, pointing in recent years to genetic evidence showing that we share some 98 percent of our genes with chimpanzees. But if our shared genetic heritage can explain the evolutionary origin of the human mind, then why isn't a chimpanzee writing this essay, or singing backup for the Rolling Stones or making soufflé? Indeed, mounting evidence indicates that, in contrast to Darwin's theory of a continuity of mind between humans and other species, a profound gap separates our intellect from the animal kind.[22]

David J. Buller's article titled "Four Fallacies of Pop Evolutionary Psychology" signals serious misunderstanding about the prospects of how the human mind could have evolved since the Stone Age.[23]

Darwinists are aware of science's limits, but in order to compete with religion, they delve wittingly into the domain of pseudoscience. However, in order to remain under the umbrella of science, they dishonestly characterize events that are tantamount to miracles in religion as lucky chances, hypotheses, or theories in evolution science. For example, evolutionary science views the biblical evidence of a transition from nonlife to life as impossible and hence a miracle or myth. However, in order to rule out the premise of intelligent causation and the need for a creator, the scientific establishment, without any shred of evidence, endorses a comparable transition from nonlife to life (abiogenesis or the spontaneous generation of life) as a theory. Why are such scientists inconsistent? Denouncing this tendency of biological evolutionists, Nobel laureate Ernst Boris Chain in 1971 expressed the following concerns:

- These classical evolutionary theories are gross oversimplifications of an immensely complex and intricate mass of facts, and it amazes me that they were swallowed so uncritically and readily, and for such a long time, by so many scientists without a murmur of protest.
- We do not need to be expert zoologists, anatomists, or physiologists to recognize that there exist some similarities between apes and man, but surely we are much more interested in the differences than the similarities. Apes, after all, unlike man, have not produced great prophets, philosophers, mathematicians, writers, poets, composers, painters, and scientists. They are not inspired by the divine spark, which manifests itself so evidently in the spiritual creation of man and which differentiates man from animals.
- To say that man has left the apes behind in the evolutionary scale because he managed, for various reasons, to develop a bigger brain is really no explanation at all; it is only a statement covering up ignorance by an ill-defined term.[24]

Chain's views might be construed as religiously motivated, but in reality they are not. In 2009 anthropologist Owen C. Lovejoy justified Chain's concerns in his remarks about the scientific discovery of the fossil *Ardipithecus ramidus*.

- For years, because of the genetic similarity of chimps and humans, it's been presumed that our ancestor would have been chimp like. Ardi (*Ardipithecus ramidus*) tells us that's not the case.[25]

In other words, Ardi tells us that Darwin's tree of life is not the case. We shall next consider why analysis of brain size is not a sufficient guide in evolutionary science.

THE INADEQUACY OF BRAIN SIZE AS EVIDENCE FOR EVOLUTION

Unable to provide laboratory demonstrations of Darwinian bacteria-to-human evolution, scientists resort to measuring brain sizes and reconstructing skeletal remains, but these data cannot prove either creation or evolution. Based on circumstantial evidence in the material realm, NASIM summarizes the significance of brain size in human evolution as follows:

> Based on the strength of evidence from DNA comparisons, the common ancestor of humans and chimpanzees lived approximately 6 to 7 million years ago in Africa. ... About 4.1 million years ago, a species appeared in Africa that paleontologists place in the genus *Australopithecus*, which means "southern ape." ... The brain of an adult of this genus was about the same size as that of modern apes, and it appears to have spent part of its life climbing in trees, as indicated by its short legs and features of its upper limbs. But *Australopithecus* also walked upright, as humans do.

About 2.3 million years ago, the earliest species of *Homo*, the genus to which all modern humans belong, evolved in Africa. This species is known as *Homo habilis* ("handy" or "skillful man"). Its average brain size, as determined from skulls that postdate 2 million years ago, was probably about 50 percent larger than that of earlier *Australopithecus*. The earliest stone tools appear about 2.6 million years ago.

About 1.8 million years ago, a more evolved species, *Homo erectus* ("upright man") appeared. This species spread from Africa to Eurasia. The subsequent fossil record includes the skeletal remains of additional species within the genus *Homo*. The more recent species generally had larger brains than the earlier ones.

Evidence shows that anatomically modern humans (*Homo sapiens*—"wise" or "knowing man") with bodies and brains like ours evolved in Africa from earlier forms of humans. The earliest known fossil of a modern human is less than 200,000 years old. The members of this group dispersed throughout Africa and, more recently, into Asia, Australia, Europe, and the Americas, replacing earlier populations of humans then living in some parts of the world.[26]

About two fifths of worm genes are similar to human genes, and half of the fly's genes is similar to that of humans.[27] Genes make up only about two percent of the human genome; the rest was for many years dismissed as "junk DNA." Over the past decade, however, biologists have come to realize that the "junk DNA" is an important part of the genetic code, "home to a vast unexamined treasure trove of information that controls how genes behave."[28] Genes/DNA tell us nothing about the minds of organisms. It would be wrong, therefore, to view worm as 40 percent human and the fly as 50 percent human, then concluding that a fly is more closely related to humans than a worm. Similarly, the evidence that 98 percent of the chimpanzee's genes are similar to those of humans should not be taken to imply that the chimpanzee is 98 percent human and hence qualifies as the closest relative to us. Scientists cannot determine common or closest ancestors based on the strength of DNA comparison. DNA and brain-size comparisons are not reliable indicators of relatedness.

An authentic theory of human evolution, nonetheless, must encompass not just the brain size but also the intellectual capacity of all the species investigated.

The brain as an organ occupies space, has mass, and can be touched. The mind, on the other hand, does not occupy space, has no mass, and cannot be touched. People can change their minds but not their brains; we can be out of our minds but not out of our brains. The brain is the medium through which the mind functions, and the interaction between the two is highly intricate. Because the brain as *matter* is not conscious, the mind is the seat of consciousness. Dictionaries, therefore, define the brain as "an organ of soft nervous tissue contained in the skull of vertebrates, functioning as the coordinating centre of sensation, and of intellectual and nervous activity," whereas the mind is "the seat of consciousness, awareness, thought, volition, and feeling."[29]

In order to function, both brain and mind must coexist; hence, we can only compare species that are consciousness-based on a brain-mind index and not exclusively on brain size. Hauser reports:

> Humans are smarter than creatures whose brains are larger than ours (human brain 1,350 grams) in absolute terms, such as killer whales (killer whale brain 5,620 grams), as well as those animals whose brains are larger than ours in relative terms (that is, relative to body size), such as shrews (Etruscan shrew brain 0.1 gram). Thus, size alone does not explain the uniqueness of the human mind.[30]

Based on the above data, a killer whale has a brain about four times larger than that of humans, but in range of function it is far inferior to that of human beings. The different sizes of brain do not correlate with the alleged evolutionary progression from simple to complex. In addition, the dissimilarities between humans and whales or shrews in the material and immaterial realms outweigh the similarities. Clearly Darwin, both on physical and metaphysical grounds, did not have all the necessary information to develop a theory of evolution or generate a tree of life. A real tree of life must reflect the dual characteristics of organisms. Data based on lifeless organisms are bound to mislead.

Things that evolve can only do so materially. Because the mind has no substance or form, it is outside the limits of science to address either its creation or its evolution. Accordingly, any theory on the evolution of mind is an embodiment of pseudoscientific speculation. A brain-mind index in the context of science is virtually impossible to attain. This limits science in studies of the origin of species. In order to override this hurdle, Darwinists believe they can blend the physical and metaphysical as one. Doing so is not only contrary to the spirit of science but also defies common sense, because no one perceives matter and nonmatter as similar in content or structure.

Let us, for the sake of argument, assume that the mind as an entity evolved. If that were the case, the nature and characteristics of species in the world would be different if their brains and minds evolved either as a unit or separately. Theories on the origin of species, under these circumstances, must explain both the material and nonmaterial sequence of events. The Darwinian theory falls short of fulfilling this requirement and hence is wrong, as the following paragraphs will illustrate.

For many decades, basing their thinking on Darwin's premise of bacteria-to-human evolution, scientists have claimed that humans evolved from apes. Many people have come to believe this myth as a scientific fact, and apparently some mainstream religious organizations are realigning their beliefs to conform to evolutionary dogma. However, in 2009 an international team of scientists, after careful study of a collection of fossils and painstaking reconstruction of the skeletal remains of *Ardipithecus ramidus*, nicknamed Ardi, conceded that the view that humans evolved from chimps is wrong. The American Association for the Advancement of Science (AAAS) news release reports:

> Until now, researchers have generally assumed that chimpanzees, gorillas, and other modern African apes have retained many of the traits of the last ancestor they shared with humans—in other words, this presumed ancestor was thought to be much more chimpanzee-like than human-like.
>
> Overall, the findings suggest that hominids and African apes have each followed different evolutionary pathways, and we can no longer consider chimps as "proxies" for our last common ancestor.[31]

Accordingly, living chimpanzees and gorillas are the wrong models for understanding the Darwinian bacteria-to-human evolution. An excerpt from a Kent State University publication by Emily Vincent states:

> Throw out all those posters and books that depict an ape evolving into a human being, says Kent State University Professor of Anthropology Dr. C. Owen Lovejoy. An internationally recognized biological anthropologist who specializes in the study of human origins, Lovejoy is one of the primary authors who revealed their research findings today on *Ardipithecus ramidus*, a hominid species that lived 4.4 million years ago in what is now Ethiopia.

"People often think we evolved from apes, but no, apes in many ways evolved from us," Lovejoy said.[32]

The consequences of the above conclusion are grave for evolutionary biology. Evolution is a journey from simple to complex organization. NASIM thus claims, "Study of all the forms of evidence … led to the conclusion that humans evolved from ancestral primates."[33] NASIM's position is consistent with Darwin's view that the progenitors of man were ape-like.[34] Darwin argues:

> If the anthropomorphous apes be admitted to form a natural subgroup, then as man agrees with them, not only in all those characters which he possesses in common with the whole Catarhine group, but in other peculiar characters, such as the absence of a tail and of callosities, and in general appearance, we may infer that some ancient member of the anthropomorphous subgroup gave birth to man. It is not probable that, through the law of analogous variation, a member of one of the other lower subgroup should have given rise to a manlike creature, resembling the higher anthropomorphous apes in so many respects. No doubt man, in comparison with most of his allies, has undergone an extraordinary amount of modification, chiefly in consequence of the great development of his brain and his erect position; nevertheless, we should bear in mind that he "is but one of several exceptional forms of primates."[35]

If, according to the above information on Ardi, apes evolved from humans or humanlike ancestors, NASIM's claim that "humans evolved from ancestral primates" is grossly misleading; also, the new evidence that "apes in many ways evolved from us" suggests a journey from more complex to less complex organization. Based on Darwinian evolution, humans have bigger brains than chimps because the former evolved from the latter; if the reverse is the case, logically we would expect chimpanzees to be the ones with bigger brains. This, however, is contrary to empirical evidence. Evolutionists do not seem to understand the fatal implications of findings that indicate a separate development of humans and chimps.

This conclusion brings evolutionists significantly closer to creationists' assertion that the species were created independently. If humans and chimps evolved independently, then the whole exercise of comparing their brain sizes in order to establish a trend of common evolution is nonsensical. Nonetheless, some evolutionists still insist on their conviction that humans evolved humans evolved from simian ancestors.

For instance, in a February 2010 cover story titled "The Naked Truth," the editors of *Scientific American*, the same journal that published the findings about Ardi in October 2009, posited that "Humans are the only primate species that has mostly naked skin. ... The evolution of hairlessness helped to set the stage for the emergence of large brains and symbolic thought."[36] Nina G. Jablonski, the author of this story, argues from the premise that "Because humans are the only primates that lack coats ... something must have happened since our hominid lineage diverged from the line leading to our closest living relative, the chimpanzee."[37] Jablonski presupposes that humans evolved from apes, a view that some evolutionists now believe is false. Clearly she and the editors of *Scientific American* are not in agreement with Lovejoy and the international team of scientists about disregarding the idea that apes evolved into human beings.[38] This points to the fact that evolutionism is a belief, not a scientific theory that would be modified or abandoned with the emergence of new evidence. This belief is now without foundation, as evolutionist Frans de Waal explains.

> The idea in anthropology is that the last common ancestor is the chimp, a fighter and killer, so we have been doing it for 6-million years and chimps have been doing it for 6-million years. ... If the last common ancestor was not a chimp, then the story changes, and it opens up whole new ways of thinking about the human evolutionary story.[39]

Scientists are supposed to shed light, not confuse the public by presenting philosophical opinions as scientific facts. To spare students from further pseudoscientific falsehood, it would be prudent for all institutions of learning to scrap the Darwinian theory of evolution from science curricula. "If an idea is out of the reach of experimentation, it cannot qualify as a theory. If the theory can never be tested, then it is no longer within the realm of scientific inquiry."[40] In science theories are based on facts in the physical world. Darwinian evolution is the only exception where a theory has been developed based on beliefs about the unknown past and then elaborated as a scientific fact on the strength of circumstantial evidence that is sometimes contrary to common sense.

When we rely on circumstantial evidence and limit our analysis to the material realm, the conclusions reached are bound to be equivocal. When scientists, based on one set of circumstantial evidence, conclude that humans evolved from apes and then, based on another set of circumstantial evidence, decide that apes and humans evolved independently, the credibility of Darwin's theory suffers a double blow. The theory nevertheless survives because of its philosophical implications. Scientists in distinguished positions such as the National Academy of Sciences and Institute of Medicine make all sorts of assumptions, extrapolations, and arguments to prevent the Darwinian theory's demise.

In its endless effort to defend the Darwinian theory's validity, for instance, NASIM purports the following:

> Many scientific theories are so well established that no new evidence is likely to alter them substantially. For example, no new evidence will demonstrate that the Earth does not orbit around the Sun (heliocentric theory), or that living things are not made of cells (cell theory), that matter is not composed of atoms, or that the surface of the Earth is not divided into solid plates that have moved over geological timescale (the theory of plate tectonics). Like these other foundational scientific theories, the theory of evolution is supported by so many observations and confirming experiments that scientists are confident that the basic components of the theory will not be overturned by new evidence.[41]

The heliocentric theory, cell theory, the atomic theory, and the theory of plate tectonics are accepted by all scientists—creationists, evolutionists, and theistic evolutionists—because they do not address the origin of the earth and living things. No scientists oppose the idea of bacteria-to-bacteria evolution because it can be tested and the results reproduced. The alleged events of bacteria-to-human evolution, however, cannot be tested and repeated.

The findings about Ardi, approximately one million years older than the chimpanzee "Lucy" from which humans supposedly descended, challenges NASIM's view of evolution as a true scientific theory. When the focus is on dissimilarities in both the physical and metaphysical realms, the only logical conclusion is that humans and apes developed independently without reference to any common ancestor. The new scientific evidence concerning Ardi confirms that the two species developed through very different evolutionary pathways and that "the ancestor is not transitional between apes and humans."[42]

If transitions from one type of organism to another occurred in the past, samples of similar transitions should be evident in the living world. Is it by chance that all of the alleged common ancestors are extinct? Because these creatures never existed, there is nothing to test in order to validate them as a scientific hypothesis. The notion of missing links, as I explained in *The Darwinian Delusion*, is a myth. The findings regarding Ardi support *New Scientist's* cover story, "Darwin Was Wrong: Cutting Down the Tree of Life," which was published on the eve of Darwin's bicentenary.[43]

The scientific community's reaction to this article is instructive. Leading evolutionists took umbrage at *New Scientist* and called for a boycott of the publication.[44] Fortunately *New Scientist*, which was founded by nuclear physicists, is not a peer-reviewed scientific journal and thus not swayed by the regnant dogmatism. For this reason creationist researchers rarely get their work published in major scientific journals that are peer-reviewed. This pattern also suggests that Darwinism is a delusion masquerading as science.

THE COMPUTER SYSTEM AND OTHER ANALOGIES

Analogical reasoning is a valuable scientific procedure; Darwin's bacteria-to-human theory of evolution leaned heavily on analogy in summing and defending his views. He wrote:

> **Analogy** would lead me one step further, namely, to the belief that all animals and plants have descended from some one prototype. But **analogy** may be a deceitful guide. Nevertheless all living things have much in common, in their chemical composition, their germinal vesicles, their cellular structure, and their laws of growth and reproduction. … Therefore I should infer from **analogy** that probably all the organic beings which have ever lived on this earth have descended from some one primordial form, into which life was first breathed.[45] (Emphasis mine.)

Analogy is a credible guide in understanding the relationship between the mind and the brain. The computer system provides a useful analogy to the matter-mind dualism in biological science. The Central Processing Unit (CPU) of a computer system is comparable to the human brain, and its software is comparable to the human mind. Any description of a computer system would be incomplete without reference to both its hardware and its software. In like manner, a complete description of the human species must involve both body and mind. Just as a computer's hardware and software are autonomous but both are required for the system to function properly, so the brain and mind are interdependent.

Programmers formulate instructions that run the computer system in the form of a binary code and install it on a hard drive. The computer's "brain," unlike the human mind that created it, is mechanical; its software cannot change the coded information. The human mind, on the other hand, is superior because it has the flexibility or free will to change. The computer's software information (as nonmatter) does not originate from the CPU (as matter); similarly, the mind cannot originate from the brain. A computer's hardware and software do not come about by chance; based on this commonsense analogy, the human brain and mind cannot be the product of random chance.

Science has no evidence of a process whereby organized, coded, and complex information can be generated without intelligence. We know that natural processes, which are unconscious, cannot write coded information; therefore, to claim that this happened sometime in the distant past is simply a scientism of the gaps. It is only logical to conclude that a genetic program utilizing a quaternary code is evidence of an immaterial and superior intelligence operating in the natural and material realm. Such a conclusion, unfortunately, is anathema to Darwinists because it contradicts their faith in materialism and naturalism. Science is about fact derived from observation and analogy. Intellectual integrity demands that we follow the evidence and not our philosophical preferences.

Here permit me to hark back to an earlier point. If, according to paleoanthropologist Tim White, who headed the international team of researchers, Ardi is neither chimpanzee nor human,[46] then the discovery confirms that chimps and humans are analogous to different computer systems with different hardware and software manufactured by the same designer using similar substances. There is no empirical evidence that one species evolved into the other, despite evolutionists' dogmatic proclamations to that effect.

Scholars also use other systems as analogies in the brain/mind debate. Distinguished physician Deepak Chopra, for instance, uses the principles behind the radio and television systems to explain the difference between the mind and the brain. He asserts:

> Just as a radio picks up the signals that transmit music, so the brain functions to bring mind into everyday reality. If the radio is smashed, the music goes away. If the brain is ill, defective or damaged, some aspect of mind will go away. But to use this reasoning as proof that the brain is the mind or more real than the mind, is utter folly. Would you believe it if someone claimed that World War II was caused by Germany and Japan having something wrong in the brain? Would you believe it if you were told a spouse you deeply love and trust only appeals to you because prehistoric man needed to bunch up by the fire in order not to freeze?[47]
>
> To gain credibility, the mind outside the brain must also be mirrored inside the brain. If your brain didn't register what the mind is doing, there would be no way to detect the mind. Like a TV program being broadcast in the air, a receiver picks up the signal and makes it visible. The brain is a receiver for the mind field. The field itself is invisible,

but as mirrored in our brains, it comes to life as images, sensations, and an infinite array of experiences.⁴⁸

In conformity with Chopra's views, Thais Campos argues:

> The television does not create the images it shows and the radio does not create the music it plays – they are just machines projected to capture the waves that are passing through the air. If you destroy the radio device, you won't be able to listen to music, but you haven't destroyed the music, it exists independently from the machine that captures it, right?
>
> Just like electricity continues to exist even if all light bulbs break, life as a potential, exists without the bodies, and the mind exists without the brain.⁴⁹

Using a car and driver as his analogy, Lawyer Victor J. Zammit, a retired attorney of the Supreme Court of the New South Wales and the High Court of Australia, in his article "The Mind/ Brain Debate in the Age of Science" wrote:

> The mind can be seen as the driver of a motor car and the brain as the car itself. The brain obeys the mind. The mind gives direction and continues to accumulate all the experiences. When the car rusts and 'dies', the driver mind lives on.⁵⁰

In Zammit's analogy, we notice that a car's key is a separate device; the driver (mind) cannot operate the car (brain) without the proper connection. A car will be inoperative if the engine is dead or the key is missing or not working.

Science does not inhibit credible analogies; however, because the immaterial realm is outside its purview, science cannot exclusively endorse any worldview on the origin of species.

SUMMARY

Studies limited to materiality are inadequate in establishing the origin of organized systems such as human beings. Basing their inferences on different sets of circumstantial evidence, scientists therefore can conclude that humans evolved from chimpanzee-like progenitors and, on the other hand, claim that chimpanzees descended from humanlike predecessors. A scientific theory on human origins must be credible. Lack of credibility should not only modify an existing theory but also trigger its abandonment as superseded dogma.

Scientists extend their explanations in evolution beyond the limits of science. The same concept (life from nonlife) that they classify as miracle or myth in religion is what they describe as hypothesis or theory in evolutionary biology. Scientific integrity demands that the timeless rules, such as testability and repeatability of events, that disqualified the creationist worldview as science must also dismiss the evolutionist worldview.

Not all scientific theories have been deemed immutable facts. For example, chemists' phlogiston theory of combustion, physicists' ether theory of light propagation, and astronomers' geocentric theory of the universe were all eventually abandoned. Darwin's theory of biological evolution by natural selection is next in line but is zealously defended by evolutionists because of its philosophical, social, and economic implications. Scientists must choose between scientific integrity and philosophical preference.

I conclude this chapter with reference to Deepak Chopra's brilliant rebuttal to materialism.

Is science the only route to knowledge? Obviously not. I know that my mother loved me all her life, as I love my own children. I feel genius in great works of art. None of this knowledge is validated by science. I have seen medical cures that science can't explain, some seemingly triggered by faith. The same is true of millions of other people. I know that I am conscious and have a self, even though Dawkins--along with many arch materialists--doesn't believe that consciousness is real or that the self is anything but a chemical illusion created in the brain. By Dawkins' reasoning a mother's love is no more real than God as neither can be empirically quantified. In fact, insofar as brain research can locate centers of activity that light up whenever a person feels love or pleasure or sexual arousal, these subjective states leave objective traces behind. That makes them more real, not less. In the same way, the brain lights up when a person feels inspired or close to God; therefore, we may be getting closer to the connection between inner and outer states, not further away.

A materialist could conceivably analyze the brain functions of a Mozart or Beethoven down to the last synaptic firing, but that would tell us nothing about why music exists, why it is beautiful, where great symphonies come from, why inspiration uplifts the listener, or in fact any relevant thing about the meaning of music. The world in general has meaning, deep meaning at times. This cannot be dismissed as a delusion, an artifact of chemicals. Beauty and meaning can be known independent of a biochemical analysis.

The same analogy comes to mind whenever one hears that brain research will eventually explain all human thought and behavior. If a scientist could map every molecule in a radio as it was playing the Beethoven Fifth, there would be a complete diagram of the symphony at the level of matter. But the radio isn't Beethoven. It isn't his mind, and a diagram of Beethoven's brain, which would also be at the level of matter, is equally futile to explain what is mind was like except in the crudest terms.[51]

At the empirical level, science constrains both the creation and evolution worldviews on the origin of species.

CHAPTER 2

CREATIONISM AND EVOLUTIONISM COMPARED

In accepting evolution as a fact, how many biologists pause to reflect that science is built upon theories that have been proved by experiment to be correct, or remember that the theory of animal evolution has never been thus proved? ... The fact of evolution is the backbone of biology, and biology is thus in the peculiar position of being a science founded on an unproved theory—is it then a science or a faith? Belief in the theory of evolution is thus exactly parallel to belief in special creation—both are concepts which believers know to be true but neither, up to the present, has been capable of proof.[1]

—L. Harrison Matthews

The establishment of evolution is not based on tested or repeatable observations but rather on a philosophical interpretation and assumptions. ... One must realize that the idea of evolution is no more a proven fact than the idea of creation. ... To teach assumptions and philosophical bias as scientific truth is misleading education and deprives individuals from making the choice themselves.[2]

—Editorial staff, The *Forerunner*

One morning I asked one of my colleagues whether she believed Darwin's story about human evolution. She paused and said, "Yes, because I believe in change over time." If this is what Darwinian evolution is all about, natural events such as aging are an evolutionary event. For a more correct understanding of the ongoing dispute regarding the origin of species, we must distinguish between facts and beliefs. Scholars mislead the public by presenting the conflict as the "creation-evolution controversy" instead of the "creationism-evolutionism controversy."

The controversy within the scientific community is not between creation (inventing or producing new things from other things; for instance, proteins are naturally created out of amino acids) and evolution (modifying things with time; for instance, when treated with antibiotics, bacteria change from resistant to nonresistant species). Accordingly, creation and evolution are facts of life and processes in science. Instead, the controversy within the scientific community is philosophical and concerns creationism versus evolutionism, which are different beliefs about the origin and diversity of life on planet Earth.[3]

Confusion arises from the fact that the scientific establishment and the media present creationism as a religious paradigm and evolutionism as a scientific paradigm. For this reason, we need to distinguish between evolution and the dogma of evolutionism. In events such as bacteria-to-bacteria evolution, there is modification without transformation. Because the events are observable and repeatable, they fall within the limits of science. Evolutionism, however, denotes the bacteria-to-human model that Darwin and his disciples theorize. This concept involves numerous transformations that are not observable or testable in the physical world; hence, it is outside the limits of science. Current school curricula present evolution as both science and pseudoscience.

EVOLUTION VERSUS CREATION AS NATURAL PROCESSES

Creation constitutes a primary process, whereas evolution is a secondary process since it presupposes the existence of raw material. While a primary process may trigger a secondary process, the reverse is impossible. Evolution modifies only the basic forms of organisms. Accordingly, any true account of the origin of life must logically begin with creation, the foundation for any evolutionary event. *Evolution is therefore subordinate to and dependent on creation as a natural process.* Because evolutionists are conscious of this fact, they often substitute improperly the term "evolution" for "creation" or its variants. For instance, rather than "As technologies of communications *were invented* [or *created*]," Michael Dowd in his book *Thank God for Evolution* writes, "As technologies of communications evolved"; similarly, rather than "Throughout this *creation* [or *formation*] of human communities and networks," he writes, "Throughout this *evolution* of human communities and networks" [my emphasis].[4] Such phrases are deliberate attempts to promote evolutionism to the public.

Evolutionist Theodosius Dobzhansky wrongly ascribes to evolution the following primary roles:

> Evolution is not predestined to promote always the good and the beautiful. Nevertheless, evolution is a process which has produced life from non-life, which has brought forth man from an animal, and which may conceivably continue doing remarkable things in the future. ... Evolution comprises all the stages of development of the universe: the cosmic, biological, and human or cultural developments. ... Life is a product of the evolution of inorganic nature, and man is a product of the evolution of life. ... Mankind's distinctive attributes and capacities arose in evolution under the control of natural selection. Natural selection makes the

evolutionary changes usually adaptive in the environments in which the species lives.[5]

These claims are philosophical and completely unscientific. As a subordinate process, evolution cannot explain the universe without resorting to ambiguous assumptions that science is unable to falsify. In fact, evolutionists admit that their model is outside the limits of empirical science, but they still insist that their views are not necessarily false.[6]

EVOLUTIONISM VERSUS CREATIONISM AS WORLDVIEWS

"Evolutionism is the belief in the Darwinian paradigm of evolution beyond the limits of scientific verification. Outside the scientific domain the evolutionary worldview is tainted with philosophical assumptions and conclusions as it tangles with the mystery of the origin of life and the universe."[7] Creationism and evolutionism are not scientific facts; instead, they are conceptual models for explaining the origins of life.

Creation presupposes an intelligent creator, and evolution postulates an unintelligent instrumentality guided by chance. The scientific community, like the public generally, is split because empirical science can neither disprove creation nor prove evolution to be the cause for the existence of the universe and its various life-forms. The division is not over bacteria-to-bacteria evolution, which is a field of regular science where the mechanisms are well known. This aspect of evolutionary science has productive applications in medicine and agriculture. Instead, the controversy is over the alleged Darwinian process of bacteria-to-human evolution, which science cannot demonstrate or reproduce.

Creationists theorize that the diversity of species is evidence of creative design by an intelligent agency using similar materials and structural arrangements, which allows for adaptations and variations that are limited to species' boundaries. Evolutionists, in contrast, theorize that the diversity of species is evidence of numerous transformations of a common ancestor under the influence of chance, variation, and natural selection. For the evolutionists' worldview to be a scientific fact, we require some form of laboratory demonstration of the changes from simple to complex organization, in addition to historical evidence of the numerous transitional stages in the fossil record and in the living world. No such proof or evidence exists, however, as molecular biologist Jonathan Wells explains:

> Most universities and public schools teach Darwinism as though it were unquestioned fact, though the truth is that a growing number of scientists are questioning it on evidential grounds. Data from the genome projects are revealing major inconsistencies in the Darwinian claim that all organisms share a common ancestor, and no one has ever observed the origin of a new species— much less the origin of new organs and body plans—by variation and selection. On the other hand, the evidence for intelligent design is increasing.[8]

In this discourse the event bacteria-to-bacteria (descent with modification) unlike bacteria-to-human beings (descent with transformation) does not produce a new species; if push comes to shove, evolutionists present this as evidence of creating new species in the laboratory. A bacterium can change from susceptible to resistant but still remains a bacterium; change in a person's immune system or sexual circumstances does not result in a new person. According to Ernst Mayr "[T]here is not yet unanimity on the definition of the species."[9] The title "The origin of species" is, therefore, ambiguous.

Creationism and evolutionism are worldviews of the same scientific evidence. For instance, data such as similarities in morphology or DNA are scientific facts. Creationists link the similarities to a common designer, but evolutionists link them to a common ancestry. Science is unable to distinguish between a common designer and a common ancestry; hence the choice between the two is philosophical, not scientific. Evolutionists, unlike creationists, focus only on morphological similarities because dissimilarities undermine their theory. When we consider both similarities and dissimilarities, the scientific evidence corroborates the biblical assertion that living things are derived from similar substances (Gen. 2:7, 19) but of different kinds or quality ("All flesh is not the same; humans have one kind of flesh, beasts have another, birds another, and fish another" [1 Cor. 15: 39]). This confirms that the flesh of organisms has not evolved. Evolutionists' choice of a common ancestry over an intelligent designer, is, therefore, primarily motivated by preference and not based on the realities of our world.

Science cannot contradict truth, but scientists can when they operate outside the limits of science. Science is all about timeless natural processes and events. It does not rely on alleged processes or events of the past that no longer exist, such as the purported emergence of life from nonlife. We know that in industries the progression from simple to complex organization is invariably the product of intelligence. The question of when DNA came into existence is not a biological issue but an historical question. How evolutionism crosses the boundaries of science is evident in the words of Pierre Teilhard de Chardin, who describes it as a "movement whose orbit infinitely transcends the natural sciences and has successively invaded and conquered the surrounding territory—chemistry, physics, sociology, and even mathematics and the history of religions. ... [It] is a general condition to which all theories, all systems, all hypotheses must bow and which they must satisfy henceforward if they are to be thinkable and true. Evolution is a light illuminating all facts, a curve that all lines must follow."[10] These beliefs are evident in the statements of other diehard Darwinists.

Jonathan Wells, in his book *The Politically Incorrect Guide to Darwinism and Intelligent Design*, successfully challenges the ridiculous claim that "nothing in biology makes sense except in the light of evolution."[11] Wells argues:

> But if nothing in biology makes sense except in the light of Darwinian evolution, how did it happen that most major biological disciplines were founded either before Darwin or by scientists who rejected his theory? Why do Darwinists claim that their hypothesis is indispensable for agriculture, when it was Darwin who needed farmers—not farmers who needed Darwin? How do Darwinists get away with claiming credit for Mendelian genetics, when Mendel doubted their theory and they ignored his work for decades? In what way is Darwinian evolution indispensable to medicine, when the modern decline in infectious diseases resulted from public health measures and scientific disciplines that owe nothing to Darwin's theory?[12]

Science does not need biological evolution to support all of its practical benefits in the modern world, but proponents of Darwinian evolution need science as a vehicle to promote their philosophical preference. Therefore, whenever evolutionists want to solicit public endorsement, they start by recounting scientific achievements that have no bearing whatsoever on evolution. For instance, in an effort to promote the evolutionist worldview to the public, NASIM, in the preface of its 2008 booklet *Science, Evolution, and Creationism*, began by first highlighting the achievements in science:

> Every day we rely on technologies made possible through the application of scientific knowledge and processes. The computers and cell phones, which we use, the cars and airplanes in which we travel, the medicines that we take, and many of the foods that we eat were developed in part through insights obtained from scientific research. Science has boosted living standards, has enabled humans to travel into Earth's orbit and to the Moon, and has given us new ways of thinking about ourselves and the universe.[13]

NASIM did not credit any of the above achievements to either evolution or creation since they all satisfy science's requirement of testability and repeatability of phenomena. However, to promote Darwin's bacteria-to-human evolution by natural selection that is neither testable nor repeatable, NASIM wrote:

> Evolutionary biology has been and continues to be a cornerstone of modern science. This booklet documents some of the major contributions that an understanding of evolution has made to human well-being, including its contributions to preventing and treating human disease, developing new agricultural products, and creating industrial innovations. [. . .]. The rapid advances now being made in the life sciences and in medicine rest on principles derived from an understanding of evolution.[14]

The controversy is not over evolution or creation as natural processes, so it makes no sense to attribute scientific achievements to either evolution or creation. In my book *The Darwinian Delusion*, I explained:

> These cited medical, agriculture, and industrial advancements are the products of the modern science laboratory version of the local farmyard breeding experience

with plants and animals that Darwin benefited from in building his untestable "bacteria-to-human" theory of evolution by natural selection. These advances could equally be pursued under a different title such as "Applied Genetics" or "Industrial biology"; evolution and creation are generic terms. Scientists, agree unanimously on the mechanisms involved in these advances. Therefore, evolutionists cannot exclusively claim credit for these advances. ... Because evolutionists do not have illustrated empirical evidence on the alleged transitions between different kinds of organism, they cling to the observed changes within the same organism (bacteria-to-bacteria modification) as the argument that the former (bacteria-to-human transformation) can be achieved.[15]

In addition, because Darwinian evolution is founded on an unproved theory, as evolutionist L. Harrison Matthews affirms,[16] it attaches itself parasitically to well-established principles and laws in science, such as the laws of thermodynamics, and where the principles and laws contravene their tenets, as does the law of biogenesis, Darwinians override them with ridiculous assumptions such as abiogenesis.

Table 2.1 compares the two worldviews. Creationism portrays a normal scenario wherein the designer (God) claims the designed (human beings and the universe). Evolutionism advocates an abnormal scenario wherein the designed (evolutionists) by rule of preference claims the designer (natural selection). Science advocates the empirical law of biogenesis and hence points to creationism. Pseudoscience promotes the unverifiable belief of abiogenesis and therefore endorses evolutionism. The point is that evolutionists are more concerned with taking God out of the equation than with respecting the integrity of science.

Richard Lewontin of Harvard University asserts:

It is not that the methods and institutions of science somehow compel us to accept a material explanation of the phenomenal world, but, on the contrary, that we are forced by our a priori adherence to material causes to create an apparatus of investigation and a set of concepts that produce material explanations, no matter how counterintuitive, no matter how mystifying to the uninitiated. Moreover, that materialism is absolute, for we cannot allow a Divine Foot in the door.[17]

Jerry Fodor and Massimo Piattelli-Palmarini were told "You must choose between faith in God and faith in Darwin; and if you want to be a secular humanist, you'd better choose the latter."[18]

Table 2:1 Creationism and Evolutionism Compared

Creationism	Evolutionism
Belief System: Divinity. "God" is truth, immaterial, omnipresent, omniscient, immutable, and omnipotent. **Foundation:** Historical revelation. God appeared before an assembly of ancient Israelites and claimed credit for having created the world.	**Belief System:** Humanistic naturalism. Nature, time, and chance are all-powerful. **Foundation:** Materialism and atheistic assumptions. Chance and accident created the universe.
Origin of Species: God fully made organisms—some to crawl, others to walk on land, and still others to navigate the waters and sky—from wet clay and biologically programmed them to reproduce after their kind. Humans were specially created in the image of God with the commission to develop the world through science and technology and to have dominion over other creatures. Human insubordination subsequently corrupted the primordial creation and creatures, resulting in events such as, mutation, erosion, decay, plate tectonics, earthquake, tsunamis, etc. Life thus originated from God. This is consistent with the scientific law of biogenesis. The fossil record matches what exists in the living world. Organisms appear fully formed with abrupt gaps that indicate no transitions between organisms. This evidence is the "Cambrian explosion." God is the source of consciousness, moral values, spirituality, and abstract or analytical intelligence.	**Origin of Species:** Organisms evolved spontaneously from dead matter and progressed from simple to complex forms by random genetic mutations (copying errors) and natural selection, with numerous transitional links between the different organisms. The source of genetic material and the origin of information are unknown. The evolutionist hypothesis of the spontaneous generation of life (abiogenesis) violates the scientific law of biogenesis and common sense. In large deposits of fossils including different types of organisms, the fossil record does not confirm even one of the many transitional links envisaged. Every claim about the discovery of a supposed missing link has been disputed, or disproved and invalidated. Evolutionism cannot account for our spiritual values and the source of consciousness.

For the evolutionists, then, God is the problem. The scientific evidence is secondary and can be explained away by dead-end philosophical assumptions such as the spontaneous generation of life. Citing the awesome intricacy of DNA, molecular biologist and physician Michael Denton affirms:

> To the sceptic, the proposition that the genetic programmes of higher organisms, consisting of something close to a thousand million bits of information, equivalent to the sequence of letters in a small library of one thousand volumes, containing in coded form countless thousands of intricate algorithms controlling, specifying, and ordering the growth and development of billions and billions of cells into the form of a complex organism, were composed by a purely random process is simply an affront to reason. But to the Darwinist the idea is accepted without a ripple of doubt—the paradigm takes precedence![19]

These facts affirm that evolutionism, like creationism, is a worldview outside the limits of scientific investigation. The question is, "Which of these worldviews is more realistic in terms of the established laws of science and empirical evidence?" Creationism does not contravene any of the laws of science, but evolutionism does. The empirical evidence fits creationism better than evolutionism.

THE WORLD PATTERNED AFTER EVOLUTION

Whenever one points out the impossibilities of the evolutionary paradigm, the response invariably is: "Given billions of years, anything is possible." We must realize that this notion is not a scientific fact but a foundational belief of Darwinism. If anything is possible, why is creationism deemed preposterous and therefore not considered as an alternative to evolutionism? Our imagination and experience should guide us in choosing what to believe. Logically we only need to picture the composition of a world that is built completely and exclusively by the blind forces that govern the evolutionary paradigm. This will give an indication of how far evolutionists have strayed beyond the limits of science.

First, evolution is a mindless process, so a world designed and run by chance would be devoid of science because we need sound minds and intelligence to pursue the discipline. Einstein maintained:

> I'm not an atheist, and I don't think I can call myself a pantheist. We are in the position of a little child entering a huge library filled with books in many languages. The child knows someone must have written those books. It does not know how. It does not understand the languages in which they are written. The child dimly suspects a mysterious order in the arrangement of the books but doesn't know what it is. That, it seems to me, is the attitude of even the most intelligent human being toward God. We see the universe marvelously arranged and obeying certain laws but only dimly understand these laws. Our limited minds grasp the mysterious force that moves the constellations.[20]

It thus makes no sense for evolutionists to argue that, on the one hand, the universe is the result of random chance and nonintelligent forces and then, on the other hand, to expect to use intelligence to unravel the mysteries behind these mindless processes. Second, a world constructed and governed by chance has no laws or order whatsoever and empty of immaterial values. The child Einstein depicts above would find a library of utter confusion, disorder, and babel. Third, a world shaped by evolution would be prone to spontaneity and would be without definite sexes, and so reproduction in its present form would not exist. The evolutionary world would be characterized instead by entities devoid of consciousness and spiritual values as well as sexual differentiation.

Therefore, the only logical conclusion is that a world shaped exclusively by the mechanism of evolution is a myth. Its implications such as "mindless processes manufacturing organisms with complex and organized minds, coded information emanating spontaneously from debris, and consciousness originating from unconsciousness" are apodictic evidence of science's having crossed over into the purely mythical domain.

SUMMARY

In origin-of-species studies, both creationists and evolutionists encounter the same limitations. The circumstantial evidence that evolutionists use to justify their worldview is the same set that creationists use to justify theirs. Circumstantial evidence alone, however, cannot establish truth. Hence, there can be no closure to the century-long controversy. If organisms evolved from nothing, there would be neither life nor death, since science posits that life can come only from preexisting life.

I conclude this chapter with reference to John A. Davison's captivating essay "The Darwinism Delusion." Davison first presents a problem with Darwin's evolutionism, follows it with a question, and ends it with an answer.

Problem:

It is now 147 years since the publication of Darwin's celebrated On the Origin of Species, yet not a single species has been observed to be formed through the mechanism he proposed. That mechanism, the natural selection of randomly produced variations, is apparently incompetent to transform contemporary species even into a new member of the same genus. The most intensive artificial selection has also proven to be unable to transcend the species barrier.

Question:

How then is it possible for an hypothesis to survive without verification? Both the Phlogiston of chemistry and the Ether of physics collapsed when controlled experiment demonstrated them to be without foundation. Darwinism also has failed to survive the acid test of experimental verification. Why then has it persisted?

Answer:

The reason for this paradox is the subject of this brief essay. It is, as my title indicates, because Darwinism is a delusion. The delusion is that evolution (phylogeny) has proceeded as the result of external causes which can be identified and experimentally manipulated. In my opinion that is impossible because such causes do not now and never did exist. They also do not exist for ontogeny, the development of the individual from the egg. Ontogeny and phylogeny are manifestations of the same reproductive continuum.

Many recent authors have spoken of experimental evolution; there is no such thing. Evolution, a unique, historical course of events that took place in the past, is not repeatable experimentally and cannot be investigated that way.[21]

A world established exclusively by evolutionary forces is not real; it is mathematically imaginary and scientifically pure fiction.

CHAPTER 3

THE IRRELEVANCE OF THE EARTH'S AGE TO THE CREATIONIST/EVOLUTIONIST CONTROVERSY

On the sensitive question of "How old the earth is," science and religion constitute different but equally valid ways of viewing the world. Religion is concerned with the structural age, when the earth as a planet was structured to accommodate life, while science addresses the earth's matrix age, which is the age of its constituent elements. Religion addresses the architectural age, but science estimates the geological age. There is no essential conflict between these views.[1]

—Michael Ebifegha

According to the Old Testament, God created Adam and Eve only six days into creation. Bishop Ussher, primate of all Ireland from 1625 to 1656, placed the origin of the world even more precisely, at nine in the morning on October 27, 4004 BC. We take a different view: that humans are a recent creation but that the universe itself began much earlier, about 13.7 billion years ago.[2]

—Stephen Hawking and Leonard Mlodinow

What would be your response if an investigator asked you, "How old is your residence?" A typical answer might be one, fifty, one hundred years old, or "I do not know." If the investigator were to ask you, "How old is the material used for building your residence?" your answer would certainly be, "I don't know." Scientists will always have different views of an event that happened once with no witnesses. That is why, for any event to be a scientific fact, it must be testable and repeatable under the same or similar conditions. However, no one knows the conditions of the universe's inception.

Age is a relative parameter and historically determined in relation to a known and outstanding event of the past, such as the designations BC (Before Christ) and AD (*Anno Domini*). While a single age may describe some things, others may require more than one description to explain different scenarios. For instance, two ages characterize a building—namely, the structural or architectural age and the matrix or geologic age, which is the age of its constituent elements. The tallest building in the world, Burj Khalifa in Dubai, United Arab Emirates, which opened in January 2010, will have a structural age of one year in January 2011 and a matrix age of unknown value. The CN Tower in Canada, which opened in June 1976, will have a structural age of thirty-five years in June 2011 but the similar matrix age as Burj Khalifa. Mount St. Helens' eruption in 1980 created a crater with a structural age of about five years, but radiometric dating of the lava dome gave a matrix age of 2.8 million years.[3] Structural ages are historical facts, but matrix ages are ideological and questionable, as ex-evolutionist Gary Parker explains:

> One of the tensest moments for me came when we started discussing uranium-lead and other radiometric methods for estimating the age of the Earth. I just knew all the creationists' arguments would be shot down and crumbled, but just the opposite happened.

In one graduate class the professor told us we didn't have to memorize the dates of the geologic systems, since they were far too uncertain and conflicting. Then in geophysics we went over all the assumptions that go into radiometric dating. Afterwards, the professor said something like this, "If a fundamentalist ever got hold of this stuff, he would make havoc out of the radiometric dating system. So, keep the faith." That's what he told us, "keep the faith." If it was a matter of keeping faith, I now had another faith I preferred to keep.[4]

This presumably explains why evolutionists use circular reasoning to date rocks and the fossils embedded in them. ("Circular reasoning" is a method of false logic, by which "this is used to prove that, and that is used to prove this." It is called "reasoning in a circle." There are several types of circular reasoning found in support of evolutionary theory. One of these is the geological dating position that "fossils are dated by the type of stratum they are in, while at the same time the stratum is dated by the fossils found in it."[5])

The earth is the global structure for the accommodation of all living and nonliving things, and so, similar to a building or mountain, it has a structural age (architectural age) and a matrix age (geological age of the earth's constituent elements). If one is interested in the earth's structural age, it is comparatively young, but from the point of view of its matrix age the planet is relatively old. Just as the ages of our residences are irrelevant in determining our backgrounds, or origins, the origin of the earth has no bearing whatsoever on whether we evolved or were created.

Since events prior to earth's establishment are unknown, there is no reliable benchmark to determine either its structural or matrix age. Therefore, the earth is neither young nor old; it just is. No one knows the correct age of the earth or the universe, just as no one knows the age of electricity. Stephen Hawking and Mlodinow in *The Grand Design* relate to this point in their remark:

> One thing that may have been apparent even in early times was either the universe was a very recent creation or else human beings have existed for only a small fraction of cosmic history. That's because the human race has been improving so rapidly in knowledge and technology that if people had been around for millions of years, the human race would be much further along in mastery.[6]

The value of 4.5 billion years that some scientists quote as the age of the earth is based on nonfalsifiable assumptions and extrapolations. While the precision of values measured by different methods may be within scientific limits, accuracy is a different matter. Nobody knows the exact state of events at earth's beginning.

Unfortunately, it is on the strength of such inaccurate data that evolutionists consider special creation as preposterous. The earth's age, of course, has no bearing on whether species were created as stipulated in the Scriptures or evolved according to Darwin's theory of evolution by natural selection. Natural processes are independent of time; therefore, the age of the earth is irrelevant in the creationism/evolutionism debate. Some scientists use the "old earth" argument to justify the fallacious hypothesis that given enough time anything is possible. It is now time to bury the "young earth" and "old earth" nonsense in the creationism-evolutionism controversy.

The six days of creation recorded in Genesis are not a measure of either earth's structural or matrix age. They designate simply the time interval taken to furnish the earth and accommodate living things, not unlike the time one needs to order materials for building and furnishing a house. In Genesis the unfurnished earth was immersed in water with darkness over the surface of the deep. Science has now confirmed the presence of water as one of the raw materials at the beginning of time. In the November 5, 2010, issue of New Scientist, David Shiga, in his article "Earth may have had water from day one" (http://www.newscientist.com), wrote:

> IN THE beginning, there was water. Earth's life-sustaining liquid came from the dust from which the planet was born, a new look at these particles suggests, and not simply from collisions with objects that later crashed into the planet from space.
>
> The origin of the oceans has long been a mystery. ... Now, it seems that water may after all have been present in Earth's building blocks.[7]

On Day 1 of the creation week God simply ordered light, already in existence in the immaterial realm, into the material realm to mark the physical world's advent. Ensuing events were as follows. The separation of the lands, seas, and sky marked Day 2. The rest of the creation week was devoted to furnishing the earth as the only planetary environment that would be habitable by living things (Isa. 45:18). Vegetation was provided on Day 3. The sun, moon, and stars were made on Day 4 by God's restructuring the raw materials supplied on Day 1. The basic prototypes of living things to navigate the water and sky were made on Day 5 and finally land creatures on Day 6.

The Genesis account provides only suggestive baseline clues about the era and genealogy of Earth's first inhabitants. We cannot relate the age of living things to the age of the land they inhabited; we cannot approximate the age of Adam and Eve by that of the earth or vice-versa. The DNA similarities of the basic organisms indicate that they were created from the same source by the same agency and within the same time frame, as opposed to alleged Darwinian evolution by natural selection that spans millions of years. A more elaborate discussion of this subject appears in my book titled *The Darwinian Delusion*.

SUMMARY

Earth's structural age (implying a young earth) and matrix age (implying an old earth) differ. The Scriptures have no interest in either determination but clearly specify as a moral commandment that the earth became functional for habitation by living things after six days of work and a seventh day of rest as evidence of the task's completion by God. This is the origin of the seven-day week, which we honor to this day.

Science has no knowledge of the structural or architectural age of the earth. Scientists are interested, however, in the matrix or geological age of the earth but cannot accurately determine its value. The ages of species do not depend on how old the earth is; hence, the age of the earth is irrelevant in determining the origin of species. Accordingly, young earth and old earth arguments are nonsensical.

CHAPTER 4

THE ORIGIN OF LIFE AND SPECIES LIMITATIONS

The actual nature of the first organisms and the exact circumstances of the origin of life may be forever lost to science.[1]

—Ricardo Alonso and W J. ack Szostak

[T]he theory of evolution deals with a series of unique events, the origin of life, the origin of intelligence and so on. Unique events are unrepeatable and cannot be subjected to any sort of experimental investigation. Such events, whether they be the origin of the universe or the origin of life, may be the subject of much fascinating and controversial speculation, but their causation can, strictly speaking, never be subject to scientific validation.[2]

—Michael Denton

Life is the immaterial component of an organism, which enables a material body to develop and reproduce. Separation of life from the body results in death. Therefore, just as scientists cannot separate the origin of an organism's mind (immaterial) from the origin of its brain (material), or the origin of genetic information (immaterial) from the origin of DNA (material), so also scientists cannot separate the origin of life (immaterial) from the origin of species (material). Accordingly, if the exact circumstances of the origin of life are forever lost to science, it follows that the exact circumstances of the origin of species are forever lost as well. Darwin and his disciples cannot, on the one hand, claim to have no exact knowledge of the origin of life[3] but, on the other hand, claim to know as a scientific fact the origin of species.

A good analogy is the determination of an object's speed through measurements of distance as a function of time. (From the perception viewpoint time is an emergent concept that our mind creates.[4]) In speed measurement the independent variable is time (an immaterial dimension), and the dependent variable is distance (a material dimension). In the Cartesian coordinate system, values are normally specified in ordered pairs (independent variable, dependent variable). For the case in question it would be (*time, distance*), meaning that we first measure time and then the corresponding distance. If the time parameter is unknown, one cannot determine distance as a function of time. If, on the other hand, one makes distance the independent variable and time the dependent variable, the result will be meaningless, as it has no practical significance in the way we understand speed. A similar argument can be made for the origin of species and the origin of life. Here life (the immaterial component) is appropriately the independent variable and species (material component) the dependent variable. If one does not establish the origin of life first, it is virtually impossible to establish correctly the origin of species. If, on the other hand, we make the origin of species the independent variable and the origin of life the dependent variable, because it is life that characterizes species and not the other way around, the result would make no sense, which is what Darwinists are doing by developing a theory of the origin of species without first solving the problem of the origin of life. This is another example of straying beyond science's limits in the extrapolation of data. A full and accurate description of the origin of species demands sound knowledge of the origin of life, inasmuch as it is the veridical clue to whether species evolved by chance or are the products of an intelligent agency.

The scientific community generally disregards creationists' arguments because they view them as based on unverifiable hypotheses. On the other hand, although evolutionists can provide testable explanations for bacteria-to-bacteria evolution, they are unable to do so for the Darwinian model of bacteria-to-human evolution. Evolutionists still appeal for time on the order of millions of years and maintain that their views are scientific facts. Rather than accept such limitations, the evolutionist establishment has set up a foundation to exonerate its preconceptions. The panel's declared mission and goal are as follows:

1. The Origin-of-Science Foundation, Inc. is a science and education foundation encouraging the pursuit of natural-process explanations and mechanisms within nature. The Foundation's main thrust is to encourage interdisciplinary, multi-institutional research projects by theoretical biophysicists and origin-of-life researchers specifically into the origin of genetic information/instructions/ message/ recipe in living organisms. By what mechanism did initial genetic code arise in nature?
2. "The Origin-of-Life Prize" ® (hereafter called "the Prize") will be awarded for proposing a highly plausible natural-process mechanism for the spontaneous rise of *genetic instructions* in nature sufficient to give rise to life. To win, the explanation must be consistent with empirical biochemical, kinetic, and thermodynamic concepts as further delineated herein, and be published in a well-respected, peer-reviewed science journal(s).

3. The one-time Origin-of-Life Prize will be paid to the winner(s) as a twenty-year annuity in hopes of discouraging theorists' immediate retirement from productive careers. The Origin-of-Life Prize annuity consists of $50,000 (US) per year for twenty consecutive years, totalling one million dollars in payments. The payments are made directly to the winner(s), not to or through their institutions.
4. Other than announcements in scientific journals, the Prize will not be publicly advertised in lay media. The Origin-of-Life Science Foundation, Inc. wishes to keep the project as quiet as possible *within the scientific community*. No media interviews will be granted until after the Prize is won.[5] (Emphasis theirs)

The establishment of this foundation is proof that scientists are worried that the Darwinian theory pertaining to the origin of species is baseless and incomplete without knowledge of the origin of life. Interestingly, the Origin-of-Life Foundation's existence is not discussed publicly, even in special issues of scientific journals that address the subject. NASIM, with its predominantly atheist membership, proposes that life evolved from inert chemicals but contends, "Constructing a plausible hypothesis of life's origins will require that many questions be answered."[6] If life evolved from chemicals, as NASIM posits, one would expect that under the management of mindless mechanisms life would eventually cease once the source/ conditions of the life-generating chemicals ceased/ changed.

The scientific community becomes a religious community when dogmatic choices become the rule and when preferences guide the interpretation of facts. Scott Todd's assertion that "Even if all data point to an intelligent designer, such an hypothesis is excluded from science because it is not naturalistic"[7] is evidence of scientific facts being overruled by essentially religious sentiments. If science is unique because it depends on empirical evidence, the scientific community would accept the established law that "Life can only come from preexisting life."

In the past great scientists such as Albert Einstein and George Wald ensured that philosophical preferences did not overrule their methodology. Wald, for instance, initially endorsed the spontaneous generation of life:

> We tell this story to beginning students of biology as though it represents a triumph of reason over mysticism.
>
> In fact it is very nearly the opposite. The reasonable view was to believe in spontaneous generation; the only alternative, to believe in a single, primary act of *supernatural* creation. There is no third position. For this reason many scientists a century ago chose to regard the belief in spontaneous generation as a "philosophical necessity." It is a symptom of the philosophical poverty of our time that this necessity is no longer appreciated. Most modern biologists, having reviewed with satisfaction the downfall of the spontaneous generation hypothesis, yet unwilling to accept the alternative belief in special creation, are left with nothing. I think a scientist has no choice but to approach the origin of life through a hypothesis of spontaneous generation.[8]

Wald won the Nobel Prize for physiology and medicine in 1967, but in 1992 he changed his initial stand on spontaneous generation.

> In my life as a scientist I have come upon two major problems which, though rooted in science ... project beyond [it]. ... That is hardly to be wondered at, since one involves consciousness and the other cosmology. ... It has occurred to me lately ... that the stuff of which physical reality is composed is mind-stuff. It is mind that has composed a physical universe that breeds life.[9]

Both Einstein and Wald thus came to share similar views, understanding the limits of science as a field of human inquiry. For science to retain its disciplinary integrity, it must respect the reliability of its foundational premises and procedures. The law of biogenesis (life from preexisting life) that prevails today started right from the beginning of life; nature will be inconsistent to begin with abiogenesis (life from nonlife) and then switch to biogenesis at some point in history. Science relies on the premise of uniformitarianism, which implies that natural processes are immutable; the processes that were at work in the past are the same as are operative today. Accordingly to evolutionist Mark Ridley, "If uniformitarianism is denied, all of science becomes impossible."[10] Abiogenesis is not a scientific law today because it never was a law. Let us reason for a moment; every game of chance begins with an input. The chance to win a lottery is available only to a player (the input source) who is outside the lottery system. For nature to have a chance, it requires an input source that must be outside nature. This input may be appropriately called the supernatural, a term that is anathema to the new atheists. So also the chance for the first life must come from a source outside matter that breeds life, hence life comes from preexisting life, which constitutes the law of biogenesis. For life to arise spontaneously from matter is equivalent to winning a lottery without playing, which is an impossibility that is only possible with the Darwinians.

The Origin-of-Life Science Foundation describes Cambridge physicist and information theorist Hubert P. Yockey as the leading scientist in information theory; accordingly, the Foundation refers to several of his works in its publications. Two of Yockey's books, *Information Theory and Molecular Biology* (Cambridge University Press, 1992); and *Information Theory, Evolution, and the Origin of Life* (Cambridge University Press, 2005) are listed among the suggested texts.[11]

Yockey, from the calculation of probability of spontaneous biogenesis concludes that "belief in currently accepted scenarios of spontaneous biogenesis is based on faith, contrary to conventional wisdom."[12] With reference to the "prebiotic soup" and the origin of life, Yockey wrote:

> Belief in a primeval soup on the ground that no other paradigm is available is an example of the logical *fallacy of the false alternative*. In science, it is a virtue to acknowledge ignorance. There is no reason that this should be different in the research on the origin of life. The best advice that that one could have given to the alchemist would have been to study nuclear physics and astrophysics, although that would not have been helpful at the time. We do not see the origin of life clearly, but through a glass darkly. Perhaps the best advice to those who are interested in the origin of life would be to study biology as Simpson (1964) proposed.[13]

Yockey, under the sub-heading, "The origin of life, religious apologetics, and the unknowable," continues:

> As George Gaylord Simpson (1964) pointed out, many authors who write about the origin of life do not realize that they are writing fiction, humour, or religious apologetics.[14]

Yockey is a Darwinist; his daughter, Cynthia Hockey, in their blog (www.hubertpyockey.com/hpyblog/), writes:

> The first thing I want noted about my father is that he is not in any way, shape or form a Creationist. He does not support Intelligent Design. He supports Darwin's theory of evolution and points out that it is one of the best-supported theories in science.

The essence of my father's work is that he has shown that the origin of life is the founding axiom of biology, just as the origin of matter is the founding axiom of physics and chemistry. An axiom is a principle that is true, but which cannot be derived or proved. Axioms are where you start. Looking for the origin of life in physics and chemistry is like looking for the origin of literature in the chemistry of ink.[15]

If the origin of life can only constitute an axiom of biology, then the origin of species that depends on the origin of life can only constitute an axiom of biology. This fact corroborates and authenticates Fodor and Piattelli-Palmarini's assertion that "[T]here can be no general theory of evolution."[16] Under these circumstances, Yockey's support for Darwin's theory of evolution is meaningless.

Abiogenesis and the Darwinian bacteria-to-human evolution are not naturally occurring events. According to NASIM "In science, explanations must be based on naturally occurring phenomena. Natural causes are, in principle, reproducible and therefore can be checked independently by others. If explanations are based on purported forces that are outside of nature, scientists have no way of either confirming or disproving those explanations."[17] Therefore, abiogenesis, a concept that exists only in the minds of some Darwinists, is a betrayal of science in that it constitutes only a *naturalism of the gaps*.

SUMMARY

The empirical evidence is that life emanates from preexisting life and terminates at death. On the question of the origin of species, it points unequivocally to a conscious source outside the scope of natural science. Biologists wrongly present the origin of life and the origin of species as unrelated events. These events are interrelated. The evidence indicates that the antecedent event could only derive from a preexisting conscious agency. Evolutionists' choice of an unconscious instrumentality over an intelligent designer therefore is based on preference and not on veridical facts.

Science, unable to explain the origin of life, is certainly unable to explain the origin of species. If we must accept the origin of life as an axiom, we must also accept the origin of the basic life forms or primordial species as an axiom. Yockey affirms:

> A great deal of effort has been expended in finding theories (i.e., algorithms) for the origin of life without success. The reason may not be that we are not smart enough or that we have not worked hard enough. The reason may be that no structure or pattern exists which can be put into the terms of an algorithm of finite complexity. ... It means that the solution to the problem is *undecidable;* it is beyond human reasoning.[18]

If analysis of the origin of life is beyond human reasoning, certainly the origin of species is far beyond human comprehension, and Darwin's book *The Origin of Species* is misleading.

CHAPTER 5

THE NATURAL SELECTION LIMITATION

Natural selection is a fact because it's a *tautology or truism*, a form of *circular reasoning. It is argued that the fittest are those that survive in greatest relative numbers and those that survive in the greatest relative numbers are defined as the fittest.* That's definitely true, but it's really just an observation, not a profound theory, and begs the question of what makes some organisms fitter than others.[1]

—Gary Parker

It ought to be common ground among naturalists that evolution is not an intentional process; it isn't run by Mother Nature, or by Selfish Genes or by the Tooth Fairy, or by God. Selective breeding is something that somebody *does*. But natural selection is not; it is something that just happens.[2]

—Jerry Fodor and Massimo Piattelli-Palmarini

The Natural Selection Delusion" constitutes Chapter 6 of my book *The Darwinian Delusion*. After citing numerous authors who have addressed inadequacies in the Darwinian paradigm of evolution by natural selection, I concluded my discourse as follows:

> A true scientific depiction of the origins and diversity of organisms cannot envision a selection process as a creative force. We have considered Gould's discontent with the synthetic theory; Lewontin's assertion that natural selection does not lead to adaptation; Grassé's objections to the Darwinian and neoDarwinian theory of evolution by natural selection; Brooks and Wiley's theory that insists natural selection cannot be a creative force; Snooks' realist theory of life in which the terms strategic selection and biotransition are substituted for that of natural selection and evolution respectively; Vendramini's "teem theory" to account for natural selection deficiencies in biosystems; and Fodor and Piattelli-Palmarini's vision of evolution without adaptation. These scholars do not endorse God as Creator, yet they denigrate the role of natural selection as a creating instrumentality.[3]

The Darwinian Delusion was published in 2009; a year later Fodor and Piattelli-Palmarini's *What Darwin Got Wrong* was released. The potential damage their book inflicts on the Darwinian paradigm is conveyed in its product description at the Amazon website:

> This is a groundbreaking attack on the most influential scientific orthodoxy of the last 150 years. Jerry Fodor and Massimo Piattelli-Palmarini, a distinguished philosopher and scientist working in tandem, reveal major flaws at the heart of Darwinian evolutionary theory. They do not deny

Darwin's status as an outstanding scientist but question the inferences he drew from his observations. Combining the results of cutting-edge work in experimental biology with crystal-clear philosophical argument, they mount a devastating critique of the central tenets of Darwin's account of the origin of species. The logic underlying natural selection is the survival of the fittest under changing environmental pressure. This logic, they argue, is mistaken. They back up the claim with evidence of what actually happens in nature.[4]

In addition to the quotations at the beginning of this chapter, the following main points in *What Darwin Got Wrong* are noteworthy.

First is the fact that "Natural selection unlike *artificial* selection does not involve agency."[5] Fodor and Piattelli-Palmarini argue, "If there are rust-resistant plants, that's because somebody decided to breed for them. But nobody decided to breed for the rust; *not even God.*"[6] Their contention that "Only agents have minds, and only agents act out of their intentions, and natural selection isn't an agent"[7] denies natural selection any designing skills. "Darwin (and, we suppose, Gould and Lewontin)," they write, "thought that he could *start with mental processes and then get to natural selection by abstracting the minds away.* But that, in a nutshell, is what we are saying can't be done"[8] (emphasis theirs). Consolidating their arguments, Fodor and Piattelli-Palmarini insist, "[E]volution can't think to itself 'frogs would catch still more flies if they had longer tongues' and thence lengthen the frog's tongue in order that they should do so."[9] Therefore, Fodor and Piattelli-Palmarini, in essence, refute Richard Dawkins' claim that "Evolution by natural selection produces an excellent simulacrum of design, mounting prodigious heights of complexity and elegance."[10] David M. Kingsley's article "From Atoms to Traits," implying that diversity arises from changes to DNA and can add up to complex creatures or even cultures,[11] is outside the premise of science. Productive and good science abstains from presenting untestable claims as facts.

Second is the fact that science cannot distinguish between the products originating from *intentional systems* (systems that are supposed to have intentions in light of which they act).[12] No organism bears the trademark of any natural or supernatural agency. Fodor and Piattelli-Palmarini assert, "Speaking as fully signed-up atheists, we can't see much difference between claiming that God selects for fit phenotypic traits and claiming that Mother Nature does. So we do find it puzzling that many of our co-non-religionists insist on that distinction with such vehemence."[13] When scientists attribute the origin, design, and diversity of living things to natural processes, they do so on the basis of a conviction beyond science's limitations, and for this reason there may never be an end to the creationism-evolutionism controversy. We must not lose track of the fact that the debate is not over scientific knowledge (scientists do not disagree over how DNA functions), because creationists and evolutionists are all accomplished scientists. The debate is about the designer—Natural Selection, Mother Nature, Selfish Gene, Blind Watchmaker, Little Green Men, or God. Nobel laureate Ernst Chain was honest in his assertion:

> The view that scientists are objective, dispassionate, impartial, and tolerant is a myth. They are just as prejudiced and emotional as any other group of people, certainly in relation to matters outside their professional competence, but even in their own fields of scientific research in relation to the views of colleagues with whom they disagree. Their power of logical thinking is also not above that of other professions.[14]

Again, it is only from beyond their discipline's limitations that scientists debate the issue of intelligent versus nonintelligent sources of living things' origin. We nevertheless need scientists to help describe the composition or explain the functions of DNA in order to reach a reasonable and logical conclusion. Natural growth, natural decay, natural selection, and natural creation manifestly do operate to affect such things as proteins and cells. These are all natural processes that modify organisms within their boundaries. They certainly are not the mechanisms by which new organisms originate.

SUMMARY

Within science's limitations, natural selection parallels artificial selection. Like the specific selection that goes on naturally during food digestion, natural selection in general cannot be attributed to intelligent or nonintelligent causes. Natural selection simply is. Like artificial selection, it is not a designing or transforming instrumentality; it simply modifies things as they are. Natural selection cannot transcend or bridge the boundaries separating species. To refute Darwin's revolutionary theory of origin of species by means of natural selection, empirical results show that new species are not formed gradually through competition but are instead obtained rapidly through collaboration.[15]

Why then are evolutionists, with a steadily growing population of agnostics and atheists, insistent that natural selection remains the main mechanism behind the origin and diversity of species? Andrew Mcintosh explains "If a scientist does not believe in God, then his starting point of atheism will be bound to affect his judgment as he looks at the world around him. If his mind is closed to the possibility of a Designer, his own assumption will force him to adopt what to many will seem an 'unlikely' explanation for what he observes."[16] It is presumably for the same reason spontaneous generation of life has received wide acceptance after the scientific establishment initially rejected it.

CHAPTER 6

SIMILARITY/DISSIMILARITY LIMITATIONS

It is often claimed that similarities between organisms in their genes and biochemistry are evidence that they have evolved from a common ancestor. ... Similarities between living organisms could be because they have been designed by the same intelligence... Part of the reason for similarity in design is that organisms have similar demands placed upon them, which can only be met in a limited number of ways. All cars have wheels, not because they have evolved from each other, but because the car-designing community recognizes wheels as an efficient way of moving over a flat surface. In the same way there are limited ways of respiring, photosynthesizing, or transporting energy.[1]

—Truth in Science Organization

Science is the only reliable way to understand the natural world, and its tools when properly utilized can generate profound insights into material existence. But science is powerless to answer questions such as "Why did the universe come into being?" "What is the meaning of human existence?" "What happens after we die?" One of the strongest motivations of humankind is to seek answers to profound questions, and we need to bring all the power of both the scientific and spiritual perspectives to bear on our understanding.[2]

—Francis S. Collins

The concept of similarity is not unique to science. The relatedness of living things is evident in Scripture. According to the second chapter of Genesis, for example, God created man from clay (verse 7) and formed various animals from the same material (verse 19). In essence, then, all living things are ontologically related. Morphological similarity, therefore, is trivial evidence in science, but when the focus is on immaterial features, we observe remarkable dissimilarities among living things. Similarity, therefore, is not a unique index in establishing the origin of species. Nobel Prize laureate Ernst Boris Chain posits that science's focus should be on species' dissimilarities rather than similarities.[3]

The genetic evidence in the material realm shows that we share about 98 percent of our genes with chimpanzees. Based on this evidence, evolutionists claim that chimpanzees are our closest relatives. This claim, however, can only be true if the similarity levels in the material realm match those in the immaterial realm. Science is handicapped in the immaterial realm, so scholars focus their studies on the behavior and mindset of chimpanzees. In the December 2010 issue of *Scientific American*, Kate Wong presents her interview with primatologist Jane Goodall concerning her fifty years of work among the chimpanzees of Gombe. Below is the edited excerpt of her responses to questions about the behaviour and minds of Chimpanzees:

> The most significant thing is how incredibly like humans they are. Many people were really surprised by the fact they

made and used tools. ... [I]t was exciting to observe this behavior in the wild, along with hunting and food sharing.

What came as a shock to me is that, like us, they have a very dark side, and they're capable of violent brutality, even war. Communities will engage in a sort of primitive warfare that appears to be over territory. Perhaps even more shocking are the attacks on newborn babies by females in the same community.

You can have very bright chimps that can learn sign language and do all kinds of things with computers, but it doesn't make sense to compare that intellect with even that of a normal human, let alone an Einstein. My own feeling is that the evolution of our intellect quickened once we began using the kind of language we use today, a language that enables us to discuss the past and plan the distant future.[4]

The above attributes are not that outstanding to qualify chimpanzees as the closest relatives to humans. Other animals share similar attributes. As a previous pet store owner, I have witnessed different animals fight, corporate or discriminate among themselves. The behaviours and intelligent activities of different animals are documented elsewhere. For example, Johan J. Bolhuis and Clive D. L. Wynne assert that birds are capable of feats that match or even exceed those reported in monkeys and apes.[5] Marc Hauser wrote:

> Animals do exhibit sophisticated behaviors that appear to presage some of our capabilities. Take, for example, the ability to create or modify objects for a particular goal. Male bower-birds construct magnificent architectural structures from twigs and decorate them with feathers, leaves, buttons and paint made from crushed berries to attract females.

New Caledonian crows carve blades into fishing sticks for catching insects. Chimpanzees have been observed to use wooden spears to shish-kebab bush babies tucked away in tree crevasses.

Knowledgeable ants teach their naïve pupils by guiding them to essential food resources. Meerkats provide their pups with tutorials on the art of dismembering a lethal but delectable scorpion. And a rash of studies have shown that animals as varied as domestic dogs, capuchin monkeys and chimpanzees object to unfair distributions of food, exhibiting what economists call inequity aversion.[6]

Bolhuis and Wynne in their essay "Can evolution explain how minds work?" report the following research findings:

> Researchers have tried for decades to teach apes some form of language, be it by using visual symbols or gestures. But linguists generally agree that the resulting efforts made by chimps and bonobos don't qualify as language. One of the prerequisites for language is being able to imitate sounds that are created by someone else. Our primate cousins show no inclination to do this. Yet many parrots and songbirds are striking vocal mimics. Furthermore, the way that they learn to sing is not unlike how human infants learn to speak. Both children and the chicks of parrots and songbirds learn many of their vocalizations during a sensitive period early in life. They also undergo a transitional period during which their attempts to speak or sing increasingly come to resemble those of adults.[7]

Distinguished evolutionist Austin H. Clark, in his book *The New Evolution*: Zoogenesis, lists the use of clothing, fire, and ornaments as some of the events that distinguish us from apes. He discusses insects' highly developed social systems that seem much like those of human beings. Clark also mentions the use of tools and implements by insects and describes how many insects in their early stages clothe themselves. Providing an overview Clark asserts:

> Incredible though it at first may seem, nevertheless it is a fact that the closest parallel to the activities of man is to be found in the activities of the insects and their allies and not among the vertebrates or backboned animals. And furthermore, among the vertebrates the birds as a whole come rather nearer to man in the scope of their activities than do the other mammals, while among the mammals the rodents—rats, mice, squirrels, beavers and their relatives—are the most similar.
>
> So far as we are able to judge from the actual evidence, the use of fire and the use of tools were human attributes from the very first appearance of mankind. It may with reasonable assurance be assumed that the same is true of speech and the use of clothing and of ornaments. There is not the slightest evidence that these human attributes were acquired one by one as man departed more and more widely from an apelike ancestor.[8]

From the above information, ants and birds are more closely related to humans in behaviour than chimpanzees. Accordingly, Bolhuis and Wynne posit that evolutionary convergence may be more important than common descent in accounting for similar cognitive outcomes in different animal groups.[9] With fossils, we are engaged in only the material realm, hence, chimpanzees are the closest relative. In the living world, we are engaged in both the material and immaterial realms; therefore, chimpanzees are not our closest relatives. In reality DNA similarity has no relevance in the Darwinian bacteria-to-human evolution.

Although evolutionist explanations are limited to similarity in the material realm, creationist explanations are not subject to this limitation. Accordingly, evolution as a secondary process restricts itself to a similarity test while creation as a primary process fulfills both similarity and dissimilarity tests.

If under scientific criteria similarity is a measure of relatedness, then dissimilarity is a measure of unrelatedness. When we apply these criteria, the evolutionist worldview passes the similarity test in the material realm justifying an evolutionary scale of relatedness, but fails the similarity test in the immaterial realm dismissing an evolutionary scale of relatedness. Science thus cannot provide any apodictic conclusion about the origin of species. Historical/religious evidence, common sense, and experiential knowledge are required to support or negate the circumstantial evidence from science.

Albert Einstein alluded to a *mind or spirit* far superior to that of human beings. George Wald pointed to a *mind* that created our universe. Francis S. Collins, who headed the International Human Genome Project, suggested that DNA is the language of God:

> It's a book of instructions, a record of history. This book was written in the DNA language by which God spoke life into being. I felt an overwhelming sense of awe in surveying this most significant of all biological texts. Yes, it is written in a language we understand very poorly, and it will take decades, if not centuries, to understand its instructions, but we had crossed a one-way bridge into profoundly new territory.[10]

Because God can create similar and dissimilar things at will, the creationist worldview thus passes the similarity and dissimilarity tests in both the material and immaterial realms. In this regard Truth in Science, an organization that promotes science education in the United Kingdom, writes: "The patterns of similarity and difference in living organisms are fully consistent with design."[11]

Does this mean that science cannot contribute to our understanding of the universe? Certainly not! Science can and should explain things such as the structure of DNA and genetic transfer, events that are testable and repeatable. Science, however, cannot resolve the origin of life or species, events that can be neither tested nor repeated. Science may come up with compelling material evidence to support a preconceived worldview, but such circumstantial evidence alone does not address the reality of an immaterial realm.

In *The Way Nature Works*, a book written by scientists for nonspecialists, DNA is described as a genetic blueprint for life.[12] Unless science believes in miracles, blueprints do not emerge spontaneously. In the real world, any blueprint would strongly point to a designer. Collins relates DNA directly to God but uses it to support his belief in evolution. Modern scientists have it all wrong when they link DNA similarities exclusively to a common ancestor, because this would imply that the common ancestor is both the product and manufacturer. In architectural or engineering practice, a blueprint represents the mind of the architect or engineer. The building itself is the material product. One building cannot lead to another and then to another in the fashion of the branching of a tree. Therefore, claims by evolutionists such as Collins that "The study of genomes leads inexorably to the conclusion that we humans share a common ancestor with other living things"[13] are inconsistent with reality. A more appropriate description would read, "The study of genomes leads inexorably to the conclusion that we humans possess a material constituent that is similar in many respects to the ones in other living things." (The word "share" in Collins' sentence is ambiguous, and the phrase "common ancestor" is misleading.) This material element is not the "last universal common ancestor" (LUCA) that scientists believe is the most recent organism from which all others now on earth descend.[14] Science relies on evidence, not beliefs about or faith in events of the unknown past.

LUCA, in short, is simply an imaginary hypothesis. Let us here examine Collins' report on DNA levels:

> At the DNA level, we are all 99.9 percent identical. That similarity applies regardless of which two individuals from around the world you choose to compare. Thus, by DNA analysis, we humans are truly part of one family. This remarkably low genetic diversity distinguishes us from most other species on the planet, where the amount of DNA diversity is ten to sometimes even fifty times greater than our own. ... Population geneticists, whose discipline involves the use of mathematical tools to reconstruct the history of populations of animals, plants, or bacteria, look at these facts about the human genome and conclude that they point to all members of our species having descended from a common set of founders.[15]

The DNA data above point to the fact that the human race has its own unique ancestors. The Bible identifies them as Adam and Eve, who were formed in the image of God, a virtue that does not change with time. Hence, humans are not by-products of the mindless LUCA that scientists have posited. DNA variations among other species reflect their distinctiveness and potential to produce different breeds. We have breeds of dogs, cats, and apes (such as fossil Lucy—*Australopithecus afarensis* and fossil Ardi—*Ardipithecus ramidus*) but no breeds of humans. Challenging the claim that similarity is evidence of common ancestry, Truth in Science asserts:

> Similar genes and proteins in organisms are taken as evidence for common ancestry. But as we sequence more and more genomes, we repeatedly find genes which are unique

to organisms. These are known as ORFans and provide a real conundrum for evolutionists. The DNA sequences of humans and chimpanzees are 96% similar, but the 4% difference represents 40 million individual differences at the nucleotide level.[16]

Matter (body) and nonmatter (mind) must characterize any common ancestor to all living organisms. Science provides the DNA map for the material domain but cannot do the same for the immaterial realm. A mindless instrumentality such as natural selection is limited by nature. For instance, while the material aspect in artificial selection is modified within the species boundary, the immaterial is not (we characterize dogs by their physical appearance and not by their minds). We do not and cannot produce a tree of life based on species' minds as we do based on species' DNA. Therefore, LUCA cannot be the foundation of complex minds and spiritual values. A common ancestor without a mind will evolve into mindless beings. LUCA is simply a scientism of the gaps, and any analysis based on false premises will foster only wrong conclusions.

Currently science tackles the controversy over whether just a single common ancestor or multiple ancestors once existed. The root of this controversy is the fact that in the material domain Darwinian evolution is masked by the existence of both vertical and horizontal gene transfers. In the former the progeny inherits genetic material by descent, whereas in horizontal or lateral gene transfer it receives genetic material not by descent but from other organisms. One would expect that the discovery of the horizontal swapping of genes would gravely challenge the Darwinian concept of a tree of life that is based purely on vertical gene transfer.[17] Strangely, however, this is not the case. Computer simulations to fit the observed array of proteins from various evolutionary models show that scenarios "featuring one common ancestor defeated even the best-performing multiancestor models."[18]

A universal common ancestor is at least $^{10^{2860}}$ times more probable than having multiple ancestors. ... A model with a single common ancestor but allowing for some gene swapping among species was even better than a simple tree of life. Such a scenario is 10^{3489} times more probable than the best multiancestor model.[19]

In the above-cited study, Douglas Theobald "chose twenty-three common proteins, with structures that differ from species to species, to examine in twelve species—four each from the bacterial, archaeal, and eukaryotic domains of life."[20] Theobald then applied standard programs for inferring evolutionary trees from the protein sequences and compared the likelihood values of how well different models of sequence evolution and ancestry fit the data.[21] The result, therefore, applies only to the material realm, a premise that does not represent the full nature of organisms and that also assumes Darwinian (bacteria-to-human) evolution model, which has not been proven as an established fact. A faulty premise will lead only to wrong deductions. Assuming, however, that Theobald's computer simulations are valid, at the material level the scientific argument on relatedness is too weak to be of any significance. We know, for instance, that cars are similar in many ways, but this does not mean that they are related in the sense of originating from a common source. If we select different cars and subject them to computer simulation on the assumption that they are the product of evolution, the computer is bound to come up with answers based on the nature of the input data it processes. Truth in Science affirms the following:

> When genes and proteins are used to try to reconstruct the ancestry of different organisms, and how they are linked in a tree-like pattern, different sources of evidence give different results. Different genes and proteins have

conflicting patterns of similarity and difference between organisms.[22]

So, if we are not witnesses of how cars are manufactured, we will be bound to take the results seriously because they are based on scientific evidence and supported by computer simulation.

Proteins provide only very limited information in the material realm. However, we seek a model that explains both the material and the immaterial or spiritual realms. Scientists should be humble enough to accept and explain science's limitations to the public. On the one hand, for instance, Collins asserts that "Science's domain is to explore nature. God's domain is in the spiritual world, a realm not possible to explore with the tools and language of science."[23] On the other hand, Collins declares that "The relatedness of all species through the mechanism of evolution is such a profound foundation for the understanding of all biology that it is difficult to imagine how one would study life without it."[24] How can this be possible when biology is the study of living organisms and when the mechanism of evolution is evidently inadequate to address both the physical and spiritual domains of life?

We live in a world of organisms that are uniquely different with well-defined ancestral lineages. Evolution presupposes a world of organisms that evolved from a common ancestor. The evolutionist worldview is inaccurate because it cannot explain the existence of immaterial virtues such as love, altruism, and the diversity of minds. Theobald's study of proteins that posits a common ancestral source of life is another example of how an evolutionary prediction does not conform to common sense and the realities of our world. Try as we may, the notion of a single ancestor cannot explain the array of minds we observe in the real world.

SUMMARY

Because material and immaterial things characterize the living world, to address correctly their relatedness, we must consider both their similarities and dissimilarities within the material and immaterial realms. The tree of life derived from DNA sequences reflects only the material realm. For bacteria-to-human evolution to be unequivocally compelling, it must show marked similarities in both the material and immaterial realms. Animal behaviour studies show that the bacteria-to-human evolution is incredible. No laboratory evidence demonstrates how a species has undergone changes in both the material and immaterial realms while going from simple to complex. The tree of life is a figment of human imagination. Some scientists want to cut it down but cannot because it will signal the end of Darwinism. Theobald's computer simulation does not resolve the tree of life controversy. Accordingly, Mike Steel and David Penny maintain "As to how much the 'tree of life' is really a tree rather than a tangled network, the jury is still out."[25]

Conclusions based exclusively on the material realm are a disservice to scientific truth. The subject of life's origins is not confined to the material realm. It also is neither testable nor repeatable. Hence, to draw philosophical conclusions without clearly and explicitly specifying science's limitations is a misrepresentation of scientific knowledge.

Minds and consciousness could not have evolved from a single unknown ancestor. If a similarity in DNA points to a single ancestor, the different minds must point to different ancestors—a fact that is evident in the real world and consistent with the Genesis account of creation but inconsistent with evolutionary biology.

CHAPTER 7

THE NATURAL HISTORY LIMITATION

When Darwin wrote *The Origin of Species*, the oldest known fossils were from a geological period known as the Cambrian, named after rocks in Cambria, Wales. But the Cambrian fossil record doesn't start with one or a few species that diverged gradually over millions of years into genera, then families, then orders, then classes, then phyla. Instead, most of the major animal phyla—and many of the major classes within them— appear together abruptly in the Cambrian, fully formed. ... The phenomenon is so dramatic that it has become known as the "Cambrian explosion," or "biology's Big Bang."[1]

—Creationist Jonathan Wells, Discovery Institute

In any case, no real evolutionist, whether gradualist or punctuationist, uses the fossil record as evidence in favour of the theory of evolution as opposed to special creation.[2]

—Evolutionist Mark Ridley, Oxford University

Much evidence can be adduced in favour of the theory of evolution—from biology, biogeography and palaeontology— but I still think that, to the unprejudiced, the fossil record of plants is in favour of special creation.[3]

—Evolutionist E. J. H. Corner, University of Cambridge

Natural history involves the systematic study of plants and animals.[4] However, because natural history leans more toward observational rather than experimental methods,[5] and because the events pertaining to *the origin of species* were never observed, it is of virtually no relevance to our understanding of life's beginnings.

Fodor and Piattelli-Palmarini argue in *What Darwin Got Wrong* that it is impossible to have a general theory of evolution, and that the story about the evolution of phenotypes (physical or functional characteristics of an organism) belongs not to biology but to natural history.[6] They are right except that in modern terminology natural history includes biology (under life sciences) and geology (under earth sciences). Therefore, to be accurate, the story of origins also does not belong to natural history. Does the theory of evolution belong to paleontology (under life sciences)?

THE NATURE OF PALEONTOLOGICAL EVIDENCE

Fossils are the remains of organisms and do not portray the functional characteristics of organisms in the living world. Because of the absence of immaterial entities, the fossil record is not a true representation of the real world. Hence, fossils are not unique in the study of the origin of species. Henry Gee reminds us of another important limitation of natural history and paleontology:

> Conventional stories about evolution, about "missing links," are not in themselves testable, because there is only one possible course of events—the one implied by the story. ... Testability is a central feature of the activity we

> call science. ... You cannot go back in time to watch the dinosaurs become extinct or fishes crawl from the slime to become amphibians. ... Because it happened only once, it is not accessible to the reproducibility scientists usually require. ... This is not possible in palaeontology except in our imaginations. ... Palaeontology read as history is additionally unscientific because, without testable hypotheses, its statements rely for their justification on authority, as if its practitioners had privileged access to absolute truth. ... The assumption of authority is profoundly, mischievously, and dangerously unscientific.[7]

Gee's argument in 1999 was validated eight years later by the discovery of Toumai, the fossilized skull from Chad. *TIME* magazine reported that interpretation of the evidence depended largely on whom you asked among distinguished paleontologists.[8] This is grossly unscientific.

Darwin's frustration with fossil data is obvious in *The Origin of Species* when he laments the absence of intermediate varieties in any one formation. Referring to the distinctness of specific forms and their not being connected by transitional links as a major obstacle to his theory,[9] he remarks:

> The several difficulties here discussed, namely our not finding in the successive formations infinitely numerous transitional links between the many species which now exist or have existed; the sudden manner in which whole groups of species appear in our European formations; the almost entire absence, as at present known, of fossiliferous formations beneath the Silurian strata, are all undoubtedly of the gravest nature. We see this in the plainest manner by the fact that all the most eminent palaeontologists ... and all our greatest geologists, have unanimously, often vehemently, maintained the immutability of species.[10]

Darwin's only response to the grave objections is that the geological record is far more imperfect than most geologists believe.[11] Certainly this answer is not good enough for a theory that is deemed central to a modern understanding of biology. One must agree with Michael Denton that Darwin's whole argument about the "extreme imperfection" of the fossil record is largely circular "since the only significant evidence he was able to provide ... was the very absence of the intermediates that he sought to explain."[12] Good science is based on evidence and not on crafty explanations for the absence of evidence. If nature does not provide evidence, the theory of evolution is without a solid scientific foundation. Accordingly, writes Denton:

> His [Darwin's] general theory, that all life on earth had originated and evolved by a gradual successive accumulation of fortuitous mutations, is still, as it was in Darwin's time, a highly speculative hypothesis entirely without direct factual support and very far from that self-evident axiom some of its more aggressive advocates would have us believe.[13]

Denton's book *Evolution: A Theory in Crisis*, from which the above quotation is taken, was written in 1986; in 2010 Darwin's general theory of evolution by natural selection remains highly speculative. In fact, opposition to the theory is mounting from both creationists and evolutionists. The more aggressive advocates in the scientific establishment and media, however, silence their voices.

The late Stephen Jay Gould gave us sufficient reasons to question the validity of modern paleontological and evolutionary deductions. He mentioned the persistence of "the trade secret of paleontology"[14] and stated that evolutionary biologists devise plausible stories that need not be true.[15] Gould and Niles Eldredge in 1972 devised a narrative about "punctuated equilibrium" in an attempt to fit the fossil data, thereby confirming that plausible stories need not be true. Referring to their work, molecular biologist Denton asserts,

"Even the currently popular theory of 'punctuated equilibrium' cannot adequately fill in the real gaps we face when envisaging how major groups of plants and animals arose."[16] The fossil evidence in question fits the special-creation model presented in Genesis and is consistent with the gaps observed in the real world. Theories about the unknown past can be developed to prop up the evolutionist worldview, but good science has no secrets and deals only with testable events. Darwin developed his theory of bacteria-to-human evolution based on finch-to-finch evolution. The progeny of finch-to-finch evolution are variants of their progenitors (descent with modification), and hence such events are consistent with the scientific requirement of reproducibility. In bacteria-to-human evolution, the progeny are genetically and morphologically different from their progenitors (descent with transformation). This is inconsistent with the scientific requirements of testability and reproducibility and hence explains why there can be no laboratory demonstration. The event exists only in the minds of Darwinists.

Nature has the right answers. Our obligation is to follow the scientific evidence faithfully to wherever it leads. We must distinguish between science and dogma. If our interest is in bacteria-to-bacteria modifications, we get that information in science laboratories. If it is in finch-to-finch modifications, we—like Darwin—can get that observational evidence in the Galapagos Islands. If our interest is the materiality and immateriality of life forms in the present, the living world is the only place to search. Since there are no intermediate varieties in our midst, then Darwin's theory of evolution by natural selection is not true in the real world. If, on the other hand, our interest is the materiality of life forms in the past, then our search moves to the world of fossils. If Darwin's theory of evolution by natural selection is correct, we should expect to find infinitely numerous transitional links between inanimate debris and human beings in geological formations. We do not find the infinitely numerous transitional links, hence, Darwin's theory is wrong.

The geological record is vast and not easily accessible. The information scientists gather, and the conclusions they reach, will depend on the abundance and distribution of fossils embedded in the geological strata. As Denton explains, the search for fossils has been extensive:

> Since Darwin's time the search for missing links in the fossil record has continued on an ever-increasing scale. So vast has been the expansion of paleontological activity over the past one hundred years that probably 99.9 % of all paleontological work has been carried out since 1860. Only a small fraction of the hundred thousand or so fossil species known today were known to Darwin. But virtually all the new fossil species discovered since Darwin's time have either been closely related to known forms or, like the Poganophoras, strange unique types of unknown affinity.
>
> Despite the tremendous increase in geological activity in every corner of the globe and despite the discovery of many strange and hitherto unknown forms, the infinitude of connecting links has still not been discovered and the fossil record is about as discontinuous as it was when Darwin was writing the *Origin*. The intermediates have remained as elusive as ever and their absence remains, a century later, one of the most striking characteristics of the fossil record.[17]

Scientists, therefore, have all the fossil data they need to reach either an unequivocal or equivocal conclusion. To reach an unequivocal conclusion about Darwinian bacteria-to-human evolution, the geological deposit must contain a diversity of organisms. Two deposits, the Burgess Shale in Canada and Chengjiang site in China, meet this requirement. In comparison to other sites, they are described as the Cambrian "explosion of life," which parallels the biblical account of primal creation according to which God on the fifth day brought forth all kinds of swimming creatures. "In contrast to the Darwinian theory of gradual evolution by natural selection spanning millions of years, some scholars describe this outburst of a wide range of organisms at the Burgess and Chengjiang sites as 'Life's/Biology's big bang.'"[18] Of the infinitely numerous transitional links that Darwin predicted would be found in the geological formation, not a single one was present in these historical sites. The same was true for plants. Denton writes, "Like the sudden appearance of the first animal groups in the Cambrian rocks, the sudden appearance of the angiosperms is a persistent anomaly which has resisted all attempts at explanation since Darwin's time."[19] This is veridical evidence that Darwin's concept of bacteria-to-human evolution is a myth masquerading as science.

The Cambrian explosion is evolutionists' nightmare because they cannot come up with any reasonable explanation for the abrupt appearance of species without the interminable number of intermediate varieties. They prefer, therefore, not to discuss the matter. Instead, they concentrate on isolated fossils such as *Archaeopteryx*, Lucy, Toumai, Tiktaalik, and Ardi. The stories they formulate and the events they associate with these fossils and their contemporaries are neither testable nor repeatable and hence are unscientific. Their conclusions are sometimes inconsistent. For instance, with Lucy the theory was that humans evolved from chimpanzees, but with Ardi the prevailing belief is that chimpanzees and humans evolved independently. This goes to show how shallow the evolutionist worldview is. Headline news about discoveries such as Lucy, Toumai, Tiktaalik, and Ardi present equivocal interpretations as scientific facts. Unequivocal confirmation for the predictions of evolution theory can only be derived from a collection of fossils and not from isolated fossils such as Tiktaalik.

Denton, in his capacity as a physician and molecular biologist, points out that almost 99 percent of the biology of any organism resides in its soft tissue, such that "skeletal characteristics alone are insufficient for designating a particular organism or species as intermediate."[20] He cites the case of rhipidistian fishes to justify his argument. For nearly a century this species was classed as intermediate between fish and terrestrial vertebrates, but in 1938 fishermen in the Indian Ocean caught a close relative of the Rhipidistia, the coelacanth, which evolutionists thought had been extinct for a hundred million years.[21] Here is a classic example of an evolutionary "fact" turning out to be pure myth. "[E]xamination of the living coelacanth proved very disappointing," comments physician Denton. "Much of its soft anatomy, particularly that of the heart, intestine, and brain, was not what was expected of a tetrapod ancestor."[22] He concludes:

> Because the soft biology of extinct groups can never be known with certainty, then obviously the status of even the most convincing intermediates is bound to be insecure. ... It is possible to allude to a number of species and groups such as *Archaeopteryx*, or the rhipidistian fish, which appear to be to some extent intermediate. But even if such were intermediate to some degree, there is no evidence that they are any more intermediate than groups such as the living lungfish or monotremes which ... are not only tremendously isolated from their nearest cousins, but which have individual organ systems that are not strictly transitional at all. As evidence for the existence of natural links between the great divisions of nature, they are only convincing to someone already convinced of the reality of organic evolution.[23]

The lesson here is that it is wrong to draw sweeping conclusions based on limited evidence. Darwin made an honest mistake in extrapolating from finch-to-finch descent (microevolution) to explain bacteria-to-human transformations by natural selection (macroevolution). Such simplistic extrapolation is wrong in every sense. As Denton contends, "There is obviously an enormous difference between the evolution of a colour change in a moth's wing and the evolution of an organ like the human brain, and the differences among the fruit flies of Hawaii, for example, are utterly trivial compared with the differences between a mouse and an elephant, or an octopus and a bee."[24] In the fossil record what evolutionists interpret as macroevolutionary changes are actually microevolutionary changes. Darwin's fault was that he placed conviction and circumstantial evidence ahead of unequivocal evidence.

SUMMARY

Darwin built his theory on personal conviction and then held nature accountable for not validating it. That there are no transitional species in the present and none in the distant past is presumably why we see only abrupt gaps in the living world and in the fossil record. The postulate of transitional species or missing links is an evolutionist myth. Richard Dawkins, who champions atheistic evolutionism, makes this observation in *The Blind Watchmaker*:

> [T]he Cambrian strata of rocks, vintage about 600 million years, are the oldest ones in which we find most of the major invertebrate groups. And we find many of them already in an advanced state of evolution the very first time they appear. It is as though they were just planted there, without any evolutionary history. Needless to say, this appearance of sudden planting has delighted creationists.[25]

The evidence clearly depicts an absence of evolutionary history and unequivocally consistent with the creationist worldview.

Nature indeed endorses creation as the primary process and evolution as a secondary process to generate diversity within a *given kind* of organism (breeders or scientists have not produced diversity *between kinds* of organisms). This explains why we have grapes with or without seeds and different breeds of dogs. For evolution to prevail as a primary process we expect to generate fruits that are partly grape and partly apple or breeds that are partly dog and partly cat. Chapter 8 therefore will propose a creation-evolution unison as the only sensible option in light of scientific evidence. This choice ensures that scientists can no longer be classified as either creationists or evolutionists.

CHAPTER 8

WRITING OFF DARWINISM

THE PROBLEM

> Neither of the two fundamental axioms of Darwin's macroevolutionary theory—the concept of the continuity of nature, that is the idea of a functional continuum of all life forms linking all species together and ultimately leading back to a primeval cell, and the belief that all the adaptive design of life resulted from a blind random process—has been validated by one single empirical discovery or scientific advance since 1859. Despite more than a century of intensive effort on the part of evolutionary biologists, the major objections raised by Darwin's critics ... have not been met.[1]
>
> —Michael Denton

> It follows that every single concept advanced by the theory of evolution (and amended thereafter) is imaginary as it is not supported by the scientifically established facts of microbiology, fossils, and mathematical probability concepts. Darwin was wrong.[2]

—I. L. Cohen

[A]s there is no single mechanism of the fixation of phenotypes, there is an important sense in which there is no 'level' of evolutionary explanation, and there can be no general theory of evolution. Rather, the story about the evolution of phenotypes belongs not to biology but to natural history; and history, natural or otherwise, is par excellence the locus of explanations that do not conform to the Newtonian paradigm.[3]

—Jerry Fodor and Massimo Piattelli-Palmarini

THE SOLUTION

Darwin pointed the direction to a thoroughly naturalistic—indeed a thoroughly atheistic—theory of phenotype formation; but he didn't see how to get the whole way there. He killed off God, if you like, but Mother Nature and other pseudo-agents got away scot-free. We think it's now time to get rid of them too.[4]

—Jerry Fodor and Massimo Piattelli-Palmarini

After all, it is not the duty of science to defend the theory of evolution, and stick by it to the bitter end—no matter what illogical and unsupported conclusions it offers. On the contrary, it is expected that scientists recognize the patently obvious impossibility of Darwin's pronouncements and predictions. If in the process of impartial scientific logic, they find that creation by outside superintelligence is the solution to our quandary, then let's cut the umbilical cord that tied us down to Darwin for such a long time. It is choking us and holding us back. An incredible amount of time, effort, talent, and money was spent during the past 125 years to argue and defend this theory. Modern microbiology has proven how the DNA works, mathematics has proven that no meaningful alignment of millions of molecules could possibly take place haphazardly, and fossils have constantly supported the ensuing conclusions. These are solid scientific facts that cannot be denied—in favour of creation by a superintelligence. Any further denial would simply be blindfolded bigotry—it would no longer be science.[5]

—I. L. Cohen

Darwinism is coming to an end, but do not expect peer-reviewed journals to announce the message. Because the scientific community is largely in denial that Darwin is wrong and because it blames religious fundamentalists for misinformation, only formal opposition from atheistic scholars who rate scientific integrity over philosophical preference and peer influence will sound Darwinism's death knell. We anticipate that the news will come from non-peer-reviewed journals since they are at liberty to report the unvarnished truth.

The January 24–30, 2009, issue of New Scientist, a non-peerreviewed weekly publication, featured a cover essay titled "Darwin Was Wrong: Cutting Down the Tree of Life." The editorial comment read in part: "Most biologists now accept that the tree of life is not a fact of nature—it is something we impose on nature in an attempt to make the task of understanding it more tractable."[6]

Fodor and Piattelli-Palmarini published their groundbreaking book *What Darwin Got Wrong* in 2010. They write:

> [N]eo-Darwinism is taken as axiomatic; it goes literally unquestioned. A view that looks to contradict it, either directly or by implication, is *ipso facto* rejected, however plausible it may otherwise seem. Entire departments, journals, and research centres now work on this principle. In consequence, social Darwinism thrives, as do epistemological Darwinism, psychological Darwinism, evolutionary ethics—and even, heaven help us, evolutionary aesthetics. If you seek their monuments, look in the science section of your daily paper. We have both spent effort and ink rebutting some of the most egregious of these neo-Darwinist spin-offs, but we think that what is needed is to cut the tree at its roots: to show that Darwin's theory of natural selection is fatally flawed.[7]

Molecular biologist and physician Michael Denton has also expressed concern that Darwinism is spreading to infect other fields of knowledge:

> The influence of evolutionary theory on fields far removed from biology is one of the most spectacular examples in history of how *a highly speculative idea* for which there is *no really hard scientific evidence* can come to fashion the thinking of a whole society and dominate the outlook of an age.[8] (Emphasis mine)

The modern scientific establishment is apparently implementing evolutionist Pierre Teilhard de Chardin's vision of evolutionism as a "movement whose orbit infinitely transcends the natural sciences and has successively invaded and conquered the surrounding territory— chemistry, physics, sociology, and even mathematics and the history of religions"[9]

What Darwin Got Wrong greatly upset the world of biological science. Some Darwinists have said that they will not read the book. Others, based on comments elsewhere, have launched their opposition to some of the book's contents. Such a reaction confirms that Darwinism is tantamount to a religion. Just as Christians defend Jesus and Muslims Mohammed, so Darwinists defend Darwin. In this regard I. L. Cohen, an officer of the Archaeological Institute of America and member of the New York Academy of Sciences, wrote in his book *Darwin Was Wrong*:

> The majority of scientists became too deeply identified with the theory of evolution and thus considered that they were personally committed, as a matter of professional honor, to defend this theory to the bitter illogical end. This approach generated its own momentum, which fed on itself and ballooned into an orthodoxy from which there was no turning back. Any criticism of the theory was perceived as a personal insult, since their self-esteem apparently was at stake. It was no longer a matter of searching for the objective truth; instead it degenerated (knowingly or unknowingly) into the spirit of an unassailable rampart, static in position, and eager to repulse any approaching newcomer—any new ideas. In fact it relied on known "myths" and grasped for or invented plausible-sounding reasons to vindicate the theory. This is certainly not the path that science should travel.[10]

Reviews in the media, not surprisingly, have issued for the most part a grade of F to *What Darwin Got Wrong*. Michael Ruse, a reviewer for the *Boston Globe*,[11] was one such person. An ex-Christian, Ruse has previously said, "Evolution is religion. This was true in the beginning, and it is true of evolution still today. ... Evolution ... came into being as a kind of secular ideology, an explicit substitute for Christianity."[12] Ruse also asserts that the theory of evolution is not falsifiable.[13] Like some of his fellow Darwinists, Ruse amazingly does not even have to read the book to condemn it. Cohen makes this related observation:

> There are certainly a good number of scientists who now reject the concepts of evolution—not on religious grounds, but on strictly scientific grounds. Most of them are keeping their own counsel. Outwardly they support evolution (so as to be in step with their peers), but inwardly they have second thoughts on the subject. It is not too easy to take a stand against the beliefs of the majority and expose oneself to ridicule, especially when one's job and academic and professional prospects are on the line. It is only the very brave and those highly placed scientists whose standings are universally acknowledged (and thus secure) that can afford to contradict the general trend. In fact, a few of these scientific superstars have publicly raised pointed questions.[14]

Cohen is not making this up. In *From Evolution to Creation: A Personal Testimony*, Gary Parker indicated that his major worry in switching allegiance from evolutionism to creationism was academic ridicule.

> Then there is a matter of intellectual pride. Creationists are often looked down upon as ignorant throwbacks to the nineteenth century, or worse, and I began to think of all the academic honors I had, and, to tell the truth, I didn't want to face that academic ridicule.[15]

Militant evolutionists speak for the scientific establishment, promoting their philosophical preference. Hopefully, however, a minority that upholds the integrity of science rather than a personal conviction will prevail.

BLOOD FROM DINOSAURS CHALLENGE DARWINISM

Mary H. Schweitzer's article "Blood from Stone," published in the December 2010 issue of *Scientific American*, provides solid evidence of how evolutionists react to findings that challenge the predictions of Darwin's theory of evolution. Schweitzer, Associate Curator at the North Carolina Museum of Natural Science, has recovered various types of organic remains that include blood vessels and bone cells. However, to evolutionists these findings are unacceptable. The onus was on Schweitzer to show that the conventional evolutionary view of fossilization is the problem. Schweitzer describes how she had to examine three dinosaurs (Big Mike, Brex, and Brachy) to defend her data.

Concerning her first dinosaur, *Tyrannosaurus rex*, known as MOR555 or "Big Mike," Schweitzer writes:

> Peering through the microscope at the thin slice of fossilized bone, I stared in disbelief at the small red spheres a colleague had just pointed out to me. The tiny structures lay in a blood vessel channel that wound through the pale yellow hard tissue. ... They couldn't be cells, I told myself. The bone slice was from a dinosaur that a team from the Museum of the Rockies in Bozeman, Montana, had recently uncovered—a *Tyrannosaurus rex* that died some 67 million years ago—and everyone knew organic material was far too delicate to persist for such a vast stretch of time.
>
> Back then, I was a relatively new graduate student at Montana State University, studying the microstructure of dinosaur bone, hardly a seasoned pro. After I sought opinions on the identity of the red spheres from faculty members and other graduate students, word of the puzzle reached Jack Horner, curator of paleontology at the museum

and one of the world's foremost dinosaur authorities. He took a look for himself. Brows furrowed, he gazed through the microscope for what seemed like hours without saying a word. Then, looking up at me with a frown, he asked, "What do you think they are?" I replied that I did not know, but they were the right size, shape and color to be blood cells, and they were in the right place too. He grunted. "So prove to me they aren't." It was an irresistible challenge, and one that has helped frame how I ask my research questions, even now.

Extraordinary claims, as the old adage goes, require extraordinary evidence. Careful scientists make every effort to disprove cherished hypotheses before they accept that their ideas are correct. Thus, for the past 20 years I have been trying every experiment I can think of to disprove the hypothesis that the materials my collaborators and I have discovered are components of soft tissues from dinosaurs and other long-gone animals.

None of the many chemical and immunological tests we performed disproved our hypothesis that the mysterious red structures visible under the microscope were red blood cells from a *T. rex*. ... When we published our findings in 1997, we drew our conclusions conservatively, stating that hemoglobin proteins might be preserved and that the most likely source of such proteins was the cells of the dinosaur. The paper got very little notice.[16]

Schweitzer was determined to clarify her data, so she examined an older *Tyrannosaurus rex* known as MOR1125 and nicknamed "Brex," recovered from the Hell Creek Formation in eastern Montana. Concerning Brex she reports:

> As soon as I laid eyes on the first piece of bone I removed from that box, a fragment of thighbone, I knew the skeleton was special. Lining the internal surface of this fragment was a thin, distinct layer of a type of bone that had never been found in dinosaurs. This layer was very fibrous, filled with blood vessel channels, and completely different in color and texture from the cortical bone that constitutes most of the skeleton. "Oh, my gosh, it's a girl—and it's pregnant!" I exclaimed to my assistant, Jennifer Wittmeyer. ... The whole dinosaur seemed to preserve material never seen before in dinosaur bone.[17]

Schweitzer employed all the techniques she had used in studying Big Mike; in addition, she tried sequencing the dinosaur's much older proteins. She found the results to be consistent with other existing data. However, the scientific establishment was still not impressed:

> Our papers detailing the sequencing work, published in 2007 and 2008, generated a firestorm of controversy, most of which focused on our interpretations of the sequencing (mass spectrometry) data. Some dissenters charged that we had not produced enough sequences to make our case; others argued that the structures we interpreted as primeval soft tissues were actually biofilm—"slime" produced by microbes that had invaded the fossilized bone.[18]

Because Schweitzer was determined to convince the scientific establishment, she next decided to sequence proteins from other dinosaur finds. This time she examined an 80-million-year-old, plant-eating, duckbill dinosaur called *Brachylophosaurus canadensis* or "Brachy." Here is her report:

> As we had hoped, we found cells embedded in a matrix of white collagen fibers in the animal's bone. ...Furthermore, extracts of the duckbill's bone reacted with antibodies that target collagen and other proteins that bacteria do not manufacture, refuting the suggestion that our soft-tissue structures were merely biofilms. In addition, the protein sequences we obtained from the bone most closely resembled those of modern birds, just as Brex's did. And we sent samples of the duckbill's bone to several different labs for independent testings, all of which confirmed our results. After we reported these findings in Science in 2009, I heard no complaints.[19]

Schweitzer insists, "Our work does not stop here. There is still so much about ancient soft tissues that we do not understand. Why are these materials preserved when all our models say they should be degraded? How does fossilization really occur? How much can we learn about animals from preserved fragments of molecules?"[20]

Schweitzer should be commended for her steadfastness in successfully defending her initial prediction that the mysterious red structures visible under the microscope were red blood cells from T. rex. Her discovery has deeply serious implications, perhaps more than she has recognized. Schweitzer enumerates every likely reason for the presence of red blood cells in dinosaur fossils except the most logical one—the unverifiable antiquity that scientists assign to dinosaurs. Her conclusion that organic materials can sometimes survive in fossils for millions of years is misguided.

Schweitzer explains that the scientific establishment was not convinced because her findings challenged everything scientists knew about the breakdown of cells and molecules.

> Test-tube studies of organic molecules indicated that proteins should not persist more than a million years or so; DNA had an even shorter life span. Researchers working

on ancient DNA had claimed previously that they had recovered DNA millions of years old, but subsequent work failed to validate the results. The only widely accepted claims of ancient molecules were no more than several tens of thousands of years old. In fact, one anonymous reviewer of a paper I had submitted for publication in a scientific journal told me that this type of preservation was not possible and that I could not convince him or her otherwise, regardless of our data.[21]

I fully agree with Schweitzer's anonymous reviewer. What makes Schweitzer's findings unique is the evidence that she was able to detect the pregnancy of a 68-million-year-old dinosaur nicknamed "Brex." Obviously the age bracket simply does not match the evidence!

For an authentic explanation, we must consider the following points. First, as Schweitzer remarks: "On the one hand, scientists are paid to be skeptical and to examine remarkable claims with rigor. On the other hand, science operates on the principle of parsimony—the simplest explanation for all the data is assumed to be the correct one."[22] If we stick to this principle, the simplest explanation is that the age bracket scientists cite for the existence and extinction of dinosaurs is wrong.

Second, it is the evolutionist belief that birds and crocodiles are the closest living relatives of dinosaurs. If evolutionists are right that birds are descended from dinosaurs, we would expect to see numerous transitions leading from dinosaurs to birds. These intermediary life forms must have had skeletons that were preserved in sediment strata. Why are such transitional fossils not found along with the fossils of dinosaurs? Why are the soft tissues of dinosaurs preserved but not the hard tissues of their morphological descendants? This point makes the study of how fossilization occurs ambiguous.

Charles Darwin and modern evolutionists attribute the absence of the numerous transitions leading from dinosaurs to birds to the imperfection of the geologic strata. But how can this be? On one hand, the geologic stratum is able to preserve microscopic details of dinosaurs' soft tissues. On the other hand, the same geologic stratum is unable to preserve any microscopic or macroscopic details of the numerous intermediate varieties produced during the dinosaur-to-bird transformations because of imperfection. It is absurd to believe that imperfection is the reason for the lack of evidence.

The only logical conclusions one can draw from Schweitzer's findings are twofold. First, dinosaurs did exist at some point; however, their history and antiquity are outside the purview of science. Confirmation of this idea is the evidence that dinosaurs ate grass contrary to evolutionists' prediction.[23] Controversial support comes from evidence that human footprints have been found alongside dinosaur tracks.[24] Second, the alleged scenario of dinosaur-to-bird evolution is false. The absence of intermediate stages in the fossil record is evidence that they never existed. The empirical evidence of their absence cannot be wrong, but Darwin's theory of evolution can.

The scientific problem is not to understand how organic materials can survive in fossils for millions of years. This line of thinking would simply try to make the evidence fit Darwin's theory of evolution. The challenge instead is either to discard completely Darwin's theory of evolution, as some scientists have recently urged,[25] or to modify it to fit the evidence.

DEFEATING DARWINISM

It takes only a few dissidents to subvert ailing theories such as that of Darwinism. Other authors have alluded to this fact, citing, for example, medieval astronomers' Ptolemaic theory of the heavens and chemists' phlogiston theory of combustion.[26] Linking these cases, Denton writes:

> The geocentric theory was the established theory of astronomy from the close of the classical era until its replacement by the Copernican or heliocentric model, a process which was only completed in the early decades of the seventeenth century. ... However, so ingrained was the idea that the Earth was the centre of the universe that hardly anyone, even those astronomers who were well of the growing unreality of the whole system, ever bothered to consider an alternative theory.[27]

> The theory of phlogiston was an inversion of the true nature of combustion. ... The theory was a total misrepresentation of reality. Phlogiston did not even exist, and yet its existence was firmly believed and the theory adhered to rigidly for nearly one hundred years throughout the eighteenth century. Throughout the phlogiston period certain facts were known which were difficult to reconcile with the theory. ... Again, as in the case of the geocentric theory, as time went on discoveries were made which were increasingly difficult to fit into the phlogiston theory, and the theory was modified by the insertion of more and more unwarranted and ad hoc assumptions about the nature of phlogiston.[28]

> For the sceptic, or indeed anyone prepared to step out of the circle of Darwinian belief, it is not hard to find inversions of common sense in modern evolutionary thought which are strikingly reminiscent of the mental gymnastics of the phlogiston chemists or the medieval astronomers.[29]

One thing is common to all previous cases in which erroneous theories were eventually overturned: a majority in the scientific community initially accepted the theories as scientific fact for several decades and disdainfully rebuffed challenges from a minority of dissidents. The public, therefore, should not judge the validity of a scientific theory based on the number of scientists who support and promote it. The creationism-evolutionism controversy reveals the same pattern.

The Darwinian theory of evolution, however, is unique from the geocentrism and phlogiston theories in many ways. First, unlike them the idea of bacteria-to-human evolution involves singularities of the past that cannot be substantiated by hard scientific evidence. Thus, while the geocentrism and phlogiston theories can correctly be classified as scientific theories, Darwinian bacteria-to-human evolution cannot be so regarded. Second, evolutionists exploit successes in bacteria-to-bacteria evolution to support bacteria-to-human evolution, which they posit requires millions of years to materialize. This proviso alone makes the theory unscientific. Tom Bethell thus comments:

> Evolutionism is perhaps the most jealously guarded dogma of American public philosophy. Any sign of serious resistance to it has encountered fierce hostility in the past, and it will not be abandoned without a tremendous fight. The gold standard could go (glad to be rid of that!), Saigon abandoned, the Constitution itself slyly junked. But Darwinism will be defended to the bitter end.[30]

Third, because the Darwinian paradigm of evolution conflicts with organized religious belief, many of the scientists who challenge its validity are ostracized as religious fundamentalists whose views are not welcomed.[31]

Readers are encouraged to investigate the events surrounding Fodor and Piattelli-Palmarini's controversial book. Like creationists, they reject the Darwinist view of natural selection as a designing agency. In this regard Denton's comments are particularly apposite:

> To the sceptic, the proposition that the genetic programmes of higher organisms, consisting of something close to a thousand million bits of information, equivalent to the sequence of letters in a small library of one thousand volumes, containing in coded form countless thousands of intricate algorithms controlling, specifying and ordering the growth and development of billions and billions of cells into the form of a complex organism, were composed by a purely random process is simply an affront to reason. But to the Darwinist the idea is accepted without a ripple of doubt—the paradigm takes precedence![32]

Organisms are complex biological systems. Only Darwinists believe that mindless matter can write software-like programs, assemble computer-like hardware, and run a computer-like system. For those who seek scientific integrity and the truth, it is time to bid Darwinism farewell.

SUMMARY

In response to *New Scientist's* controversial January 2009 issue, evolutionists Richard Dawkins, Daniel Dennett, Jerry Coyne, and P. Z. Myers posted a response titled "Darwin Was Right" that read in part:

> Nothing in the article showed that the concept of the tree of life is unsound; only that it is more complicated than was realized before the advent of molecular genetics. It is still true that all of life arose from "a few forms or ... one," as Darwin concluded in *The Origin of Species*. It is still true that it diversified by descent with modification via natural selection and other factors.[33]

Perhaps there wasn't enough information in *New Scientist* to convince Darwin's apostles that the tree-of-life paradigm is unsound, but one hopes that Fodor and Piattelli-Palmarini's book will convince their colleagues.

If not, this discussion offers the following points. First, Darwin's tree-of-life model is based exclusively on materialist deductions, but living systems are governed by both material and immaterial mechanisms. Even in the material realm alone, Darwin's tree is wrong. Based on this paradigm the initial belief was that human beings evolved from chimpanzees, but recent developments show that they developed independently (consistent with the creationist worldview). There can be only one correct conclusion—namely, that the Darwinian tree of life is simply a figment of human imagination.

Second, Darwin's *The Origin of Species* asserts:

> It is no valid objection that science as yet throws no light on the far higher problem of the essence or origin of life.[34]

> There is grandeur in this view of life, with its several powers, having been originally breathed by the Creator into a few forms or into one; and that, whilst this planet has gone cycling on according to the fixed law of gravity, from so simple a beginning endless form most beautiful and most wonderful have been, and are being evolved.[35]

To date science has not shed light on the origin of life, so Dawkins et al. are wrong in stating that "It is still true that all of life arose from 'a few forms or ... one.'" Science is based on evidence, and there is none to support this claim. It is noteworthy that, unlike many Darwinists, the notion of a creator is not anathema to Darwin. In fact the phrase "by the Creator" in the above quotation is omitted in some versions (see Charles Darwin, The Origin of Species, ed. J. W. Burrow [New York: Penguin Classics, 1985], 459–60) of *The Origin of Species*.

Third is the evolutionists' proposition that life diversified by descent with modification via natural selection. Descent with modification refers to microevolution, an established fact. However, Darwinian descent with transformation is macroevolution. If natural selection is the main mechanism, then as Darwin posits we should see an interminable number of intermediate forms linking all the species in each group by gradations.[36] None, however, appears in the fossil record. Because science is based on evidence, this lacuna means that bacteria-to-human evolution, unlike the bacteria-to-bacteria evolution, is a figment of human imagination.

CHAPTER 9

THE MYTH OF THE GRAND DESIGN BY CHAOS

Many people through the ages have attributed to God the beauty and complexity of nature that in their time seemed to have no scientific explanation. But just as Darwin and Wallace explained how the apparently miraculous design of living forms could appear without intervention by a supreme being, the multiverse concept can explain the fine-tuning of physical law without the need for a benevolent creator who made the universe for our benefit. [T]he discovery relatively recently of the extreme Fine-tuning of so many of the laws of nature could lead some of us back to the old idea that this grand design is the work of some grand designer.[1]

—Stephen Hawking and Leonard Mlodinow

The existence of the Big Bang begs the question of what came before that, and who or what was responsible. It certainly demonstrates the limits of science as no other phenomenon has done. ... [T]he astronomical evidence leads to a biblical view of the origin of the world.

> The details differ, but the essential elements and the astronomical and biblical accounts of Genesis are the same; the chain of events leading to man commenced suddenly and sharply at a definite moment of time, in a flash of light and energy.
>
> The Big Bang cries out for a divine explanation. It forces the conclusion that nature had a defined beginning. I cannot see how nature could have created itself. Only a supernatural force that is outside of space and time could have done that.[2]
>
> —Francis S. Collins

Two important offices in a court of law are those of the lawyer and the judge. The duty of the lawyer is to present evidence on behalf of his or her client; that of the judge is to weigh the evidence and issue a verdict. No individual is both a lawyer and a judge in the court system. A similar division of roles and expertise applies in the world of scholarly inquiry. A scientist is like a lawyer who procures evidence on behalf of science to explain empirical phenomena. The philosopher is like a judge who decides whether the evidence points to an intelligent designer or chaos. Today, unfortunately, some scientists have appointed themselves as both lawyers and judges in an effort to ridicule religion. Thus it is that Stephen Hawking and Leonard Mlodinow in *The Grand Design* declare philosophy dead.[3]

Such a stance deviates markedly from Hawking's modest approach to cosmology as gracefully presented in *A Brief History of Time*. In the expanded tenth-anniversary edition of that book, Hawking wrote in his conclusion:

> However, if we do discover a complete theory, it should in time be understandable in broad principle by everyone, not just a few scientists. Then we shall all, philosophers,

scientists, and just ordinary people, be able to take part in the discussion of the question of why it is that we and the universe exist. If we find the answer to that, it would be the ultimate triumph of human reason—for then we would know the mind of God.[4]

Between *A Brief History of Time* and *The Grand Design* physics developed M-theory, which Hawking believes is a candidate for presenting a plausible theory of everything.[5] Within this time frame also occurred two remarkable events in the fields of philosophy and science that centred on the existence of God. First, distinguished philosopher Anthony Flew, after fifty years of vigorously promoting atheism, endorsed the existence of God on the grounds of compelling scientific evidence. In an intriguing book titled *There Is a God*,[6] Flew defended his authority as a philosopher in the debate over God's existence. Second, Richard Dawkins, another champion of atheism, published *The God Delusion*.[7]

The Grand Design is in agreement with *The God Delusion* but not with *There Is a God*. In their final chapter, Hawking and Mlodinow thus assert:

> Because there is a law like gravity, the universe can and will create itself from nothing. ... Spontaneous creation is the reason there is something rather than nothing, why the universe exists, why we exist. It is not necessary to invoke God to light the bluetouch paper and set the universe going.[8]

The only reference to science here is the law of gravity; the rest is in the genre of philosophy. It is important to note that Hawking and Mlodinow point to spontaneous creation and not evolution. Wearing the hats of philosophers, Hawking and Mlodinow write:

> Some would claim the answer to these questions is that there is a God who chose to create the universe that way.

> It is reasonable to ask who or what created the universe, but if the answer is God, then the question has merely been deflected to that of who created God. ... We claim, however, that it is possible to answer these questions purely within the realm of science, and without invoking any divine beings.[9]

Hawking and Mlodinow must also realize that it is reasonable to ask *who created natural laws such as gravity*, but if the answer is nature, then the question has simply been shifted to that of *who created nature*.

If nature is cause, God is without cause.

Natural laws by themselves explain causation; they do not cause or point to mechanisms behind the events they explain. Hawking in *A Brief History of Time* concurs: "Even if there is only one possible unified theory, it is just a set of rules and equations. What is it that breathes fire into the equations and makes a universe for them to describe?"[10] In essence, Hawking and Mlodinow's presupposition of spontaneous creation in *The Grand Design* requires a law generator because no law generates itself. Hawking in *A Brief History of Time* again agrees: "Science seems to have uncovered a set of laws that, within the limits set by the uncertainty principle, tell us how the universe will develop with time, if we know its state at any one time. These laws may have originally been decreed by God, but it appears that he has since left the universe to evolve according to them and does not now intervene in it."[11] Hawking also emphasizes the following point: "However, the laws do not tell us what the universe should have looked like when it started—it would still be up to God to wind up the clockwork and choose how to start it off. So long as the universe had a beginning, we could suppose it had a creator."[12] What are the implications of these salient comments?

Imagine that you happen to examine building A and come to the conclusion that the builder had the expertise to choose any method of building from scratch. After twelve years you notice other buildings, some similar to building A and each with different histories. On the basis of your new finding, would you conclude that every building in existence could have sprung up spontaneously without a builder? This is what Hawking and Mlodinow are implying in the next paragraph.

There is nothing in mathematics or science that can lead us to conclude what God can or cannot do. In *A Brief History of Time,* Hawking acknowledges that God could have chosen to create the universe in any fashion. Twelve years later Hawking and Mlodinow conclude in *The Grand Design* that the hypothesis of God is not necessary because (1) advances in M-theory predict that a great many universes can be created out of nothing,[13] and there is already the evidence that a planet elsewhere orbits a star other than our sun,[14] and (2) quantum theory suggests that the universe does not have only a single existence or history, but rather every possible version of the universe exists simultaneously.[15] Hawking and Mlodinow posit that these findings make "the coincidences of our planetary conditions—the single sun, the lucky combination of earth-sun distance and solar mass—far less remarkable, and far less compelling, as evidence that the earth was carefully designed just to please us human beings."[16] Hawking and Mlodinow do not conclude that God does not exist; they instead maintain that the hypothesis of God is not necessary in order to explain the universe. Can they be right?

According to the Scriptures, God does whatever pleases divinity in the heavens and on earth (Ps. 135:6). God, therefore, could have chosen to create multiple universes for different purposes and perhaps with different laws (Job 38:33). Hawking does not question God's ability to do things, since he maintains that "Einstein was wrong when he said, 'God does not play dice.'" Hawking then asserts "Consideration of black holes suggests not only that God does play dice, but that He sometimes confuses us by throwing them where they can't be seen."[17] If God can choose to create, what is the motive behind Hawking and Mlodinow's new book *The Grand Design*? If the motive is to support the new atheism currently championed by Dawkins, the authors are right on track. Do recent advances in science unequivocally justify why God is out and chaos is in?

The Grand Design is an excellent reference for up-to-date advances in mathematics and physics pertaining to the universe, but apparently a good number of scientists do not share Hawking and Mlodinow's sweeping philosophical conclusions. For instance, they assert the following: "According to M-theory, ours is not the only universe. Instead, M-theory predicts that a great many universes were created out of nothing. Their creation does not require the intervention of some supernatural being or god. Rather, these multiple universes arise naturally from physical laws."[18] Consider, however, The Origin-of-Life Science Foundation's position on the question of multiple universes. On "infinity issues" it states:

> Appeals to multiple or "parallel" cosmoses or to an infinite number of cosmic "Big Bang/Crunch" oscillations as essential elements of proposed mechanisms are not acceptable … due to a lack of empirical correlation and testability. Such beliefs are without hard physical evidence and must therefore be considered unfalsifiable, currently outside the methodology of scientific investigation to confirm or disprove, and therefore more mathematically theoretical and metaphysical than scientific in nature. Recent cosmological evidence also suggests insufficient mass for gravity to reverse continuing cosmic expansion.[19]

The foundation represents information theorists, computer scientists, probabilists, biophysicists, thermodynamicists, artificial-intelligence experts, biochemists, molecular biologists, mathematicians, geochemists, astronomers, philosophers of science, exobiologists/ astrobiologists, molecular evolutionists, and origin-of-life investigators from over forty countries.[20] The foundation therefore more or less speaks for the scientific and mathematics establishments.

M-theory does not address the spiritual realm to be able to explain "where we came from, what created us, or why we exist. Hawking and Mlodinow, however, view the M-theory as fitting Einstein's dream."[21] We must exercise restraint, since at the moment M-theory is "a family of different theories, each of which is a description of observations only in some range of physical situations."[22] A truly unifying theory of everything must address the reality of the immaterial world, such as consciousness. Nobel Prize laureate George Wald contends that "consciousness seems to be wholly impervious to science."[23] Other scientists agree. For instance, fellow Nobel Prize laureate, geneticist, and immunologist George Davis Snell, in his article "I Do Not See How Science Can Shed Light on the Origins of Design," identifies the nature of consciousness, the origins of design, and the matter of first causes as three key areas where science fails to reveal ultimate truth.[24] Hawking and Mlodinow's *The Grand Design* does not address the subject of consciousness. The word "brain" appears in the book's index, but "mind," which is the seat of consciousness, is absent. Physics explains material things only, but the universe encompasses both material and immaterial realms. *In essence, then, without a representation of the immaterial realm science is incapable of formulating a unifying theory of everything.* M-theory is thus an improbable candidate for answering all questions pertaining to our universe.

The Grand Design replaces the role of a creator with the laws of nature. Based on the tenets of quantum mechanics, specifically the uncertainty principle and wave-particle duality, Hawking and Mlodinow surmise how four natural forces—gravity, electromagnetism, weak nuclear force, and strong nuclear force—could have arisen from the Big Bang. Natural laws, however, constitute a sequence of events occurring with unvarying uniformity under the same conditions.[25] Hawking and Mlodinow posit that "Laws should hold everywhere and all times; otherwise they wouldn't be laws. There could be no exceptions or miracles."[26] But how can chance or spontaneity not governed by fixed laws be their source? If laws arise spontaneously, they will act spontaneously; to act any other way will simply constitute a miracle. An invariant law can only proceed from an invariant source. Hawking and Mlodinow nonetheless assert, "Were it not for a series of startling coincidences in the precise details of physical law, it seems, humans and similar life-forms would never have come into being."[27] This is an opinion that lies outside science and so cannot be regarded as a scientific fact. Commenting on the use of laws both known and unknown, The Origin-of-Life Science Foundation writes:

> Appealing to unknown "laws" . . . constitutes a "category error" of logic theory. "Laws" do not cause anything. They are merely human generalizations, mental constructs, and mathematical descriptions of existing forces and mass-energy relationships. Even "chance" is a probabilistic rational construct. Neither chance nor "laws" cause effects. Unknown laws, therefore, cannot provide a mechanism for prescriptive information (instruction) genesis. Appealing to unknown laws constitutes a "naturalism of the gaps," corresponding to supernaturalists' appealing to a "God of the gaps" for scientific explanation. Neither is acceptable in naturalistic science.[28]

Contrary to the above point that laws do not cause anything, Hawking and Mlodinow contend that because of the law of gravity the universe can and will create itself from nothing. They define gravity as "the means by which objects that have mass attract each other."[29] The law of gravity, therefore, addresses solely the material realm, and for it to operate matter and time must first exist. Hence, gravity can only be the consequence of the creation of matter and not the cause or means of its creation.

A complete description of our universe must address both the material (e.g., body) and the immaterial (e.g., mind). Since laws are not established spontaneously, they must derive from a mind or intelligence. Realizing this fact, Wald changed his initial belief in spontaneous generation to accept a mind or intelligence crafted a physical universe that breeds life.[30] This conclusion is consistent with the creationist worldview.

The book of Genesis suggests that the creation event marks the beginning of time in the physical world. Natural laws presumably came into existence in the course of the creator's structuring of earth and the heavens to accommodate life. The Scriptures also assert that the earth was specifically designed for habitation (Isa. 45:12, 18). Thus, the fine-tuning of natural laws is not likely the consequence of multiple universes as Hawking and Mlodinow believe.[31] The Genesis cosmology also indicates that the law of biogenesis was instituted at the moment of creation of life. Accordingly, The Origin-of-Life Science Foundation is misguided in its search for how life in the past arose spontaneously. Such an undertaking confirms that it too is a victim of a "naturalism of the gaps."

Did the universe modeled by the Big Bang need a creator? Any scientist who suggests otherwise must first explain how the tiny unit of concentrated matter and energy of unimaginable density and temperature that exploded came into existence.[32] Did it evolve on its own as Hawking and Mlodinow surmise?[33] Every undertaking or any event in nature must have a cause. For instance, to recreate conditions of the Big Bang, the European Organization of Nuclear Research (CERN) built the Large Hadron Collider in Geneva. On March 30, 2010, scientists staged the highest-energy and man-made particle collision.[34] The project, which entailed immense human effort and intelligence, was launched with great expectations that may transform physics and its allied disciplines.[35] On the physicists' wish lists are the evidence of extra dimensions proposed by some forms of string theory, evidence of vanishing dimensions that could explain the accelerating expansion of the universe, and the detection of the Higgs boson, the elusive particle thought to be part of the mechanism that gives mass to other paricles.[36] The mini explosion that will accomplish all of these anticipated marvellous discoveries did not happen spontaneously. Scientists planned and caused the explosion to take place. With this scenario in mind, can scientists not envision the possibility that at the beginning of time a creator of far superior intelligence staged a similar but more sophisticated experiment? To argue that a creator was not needed to detonate the Big Bang at the beginning of the universe is to imply that scientists were not needed in the CERN experiment.

Untestable theoretical assumptions limit the validity of cosmological deductions, the more so because scientists know about only 5 percent of the universe. Theoretical assumptions such as a "no-boundary condition" and "time" not having a beginning are questionable, since they lead to preconceived conclusions. For instance, Hawking and Mlodinow imagined that the beginning of the universe was like the South Pole of the earth and then insist that to ask what happened before the beginning of the universe would become a meaningless question, since there is nothing south of the South Pole.[37] This is tantamount to telling the public that questions about what transpired before the setting up and implementation of the CERN's mini Big Bang experiment will be meaningless. Some activities must have preceded the Big Bang or else there would be no bang! Science cannot determine what existed or happened before the Big Bang because such matters lie outside science's purview. The questions and the answers belong to the domain of history.

The subject of time is very controversial in science. According to Craig Callender, "[M]any in theoretical physics have come to believe that time fundamentally does not even exist."[38] For cosmological considerations, time is relative and immaterial. In mathematics, for instance, while solving quadratic equations we sometimes encounter problems with negative solutions for time as a temporal parameter. Some of my students always look at me with suspicion when solutions like this turn up. While it makes sense to discount such solutions as inadmissible in the physical world, we cannot preclude the relevance of negative time in the immaterial world. For historical explanation we must be comfortable with negative time as representing the past, zero time as the present, and positive time as the future. If we apply this notion to the universe's beginning, we can attribute negative time ($t < 0$) to the immaterial realm before the Big Bang and positive time ($t \geq 0$) to the physical realm. The historical justification for this is found in Jesus Christ's supplication during his farewell meeting with his disciples:

> Now, this is eternal life: that they may know you, the only true God, and Jesus Christ, whom you have sent. I have brought you glory on earth by completing the work you gave me to do. And now, Father, glorify me in your presence with the glory I had with you before the world began. ... I am coming to you now, but I say these things while I am still in the world, so that they may have the full measure of my joy within them (John 5:21, NIV).

To justify his authority in making such an exceptional claim, Christ posits that "[W]hatever the Father does the Son also does. ... For just as the Father raises the dead and gives them life, even so the Son gives life to whom he is pleased to give it" (John 5:21 NIV). It comes down to whom to believe—Christ, who shares an eyewitness account, or Hawking and Mlodinow, who are making untestable assumptions about the scientifically unknowable past.

The intelligence behind a universe that Einstein described as "illimitable Spirit" cannot be fathomed by physical laws or quantum mechanics. The proper role of science is to understand the universe and not to debate its genesis. Science must recognize its limits and not go beyond empiricism in order to compete with religion.

SUMMARY

The universe did not create itself. It did not arise out of chaos by the laws of nature. The empirical law of biogenesis militates against the theory of life's spontaneous generation. External agency is needed.

Hawking and Mlodinow's contention in *The Grand Design*—that the premise of God as creator is superfluous—is misguided. A grand design without a designer is comparable to science without a scientist. Science cannot distinguish between supernatural and natural design. Hawking and Mlodinow's book indicates only how the authors have succumbed to a facile scientism.

A universe or multiple universes modeled by mathematics and physics can only be the consequence of design by an intelligent agency. Nobel Prize laureate biochemist Christian Boehmer Anfinsen agrees: "We must admit that there exists an incomprehensible power or force with limitless foresight and knowledge that started the whole universe going in the first place."[39] We conclude this chapter with Deepak Chopra's brilliant overview:

> Unfortunately, the Theory of Everything has hit a brick wall. Quantum physics lacks the power to cross the border into the invisible world that lies beyond subatomic particles, the so-called virtual domain. Not only is this the realm of 'dark matter' and 'dark energy'--mysterious shadows of the matter and energy we see around us--but all possible universes also lie across the same boundary, as well as the "zero point" where space and time are born.

Genetics seems to be riding higher, but behind the display of public triumph, biology has not solved the existence of mind, and therefore the same obstacle faces both fields. An invisible world lies sealed off from investigation, leaving us to trace its footprints and echoes.

Beyond the physical world lies the womb of creation, and whether we call it God is irrelevant. We came from a source, we are forever in contact with our source, and we are constantly returning to our source.[40]

Whether God is necessary or not to set the universe going is not a scientific question. It therefore does not require a scientific answer. The answer lies in the genre of history as we'll see in the next chapter.

CHAPTER 10

THE HISTORICAL RECORD OF GOD'S PATENT AND SEAL ON CREATION

People (including scientists!) are finite, limited by space and time. As finite creatures, we must live by faith; there is no other choice. But we can *choose* the object of our faith. We can put our faith in our opinions or the words of "experts," as I did through my first several years of teaching university biology. Or we can put our faith in the Word of the Living God, who stands outside our limits of space and time. Only God can tell us what is truly true, now and forever.[1]

—Gary Parker

I do not understand how the scientific approach alone, as separated from a religious approach, can explain an origin of all things. ... In my view, the question of origin seems always left unanswered if we explore from a scientific view alone. Thus, I believe there is a need for some religious or metaphysical explanation if we are to have one.[2]

—Nobel laureate Charles H. Townes

> [T]here must be a mind that directs and shapes matter in organic forms. Even if it does so by creating chemical mechanisms to carry out the task with autonomy, this artist will be the ultimate cause of those forms existing in matter. This artist is God, and nature is God's handiwork.[3]
>
> —Robert Augros and George Stanciu

CREATION-EVOLUTION UNISON— THE UNBIASED OPTION

The term "creation" presupposes a creator, and the term "evolution" presupposes none. Therefore, just as we do not designate as either creation or evolution the changes that food undergoes during digestion, so should reference to changes that species undergo avoid any slanted implication. So instead of saying that a colony of bacteria *evolved* into a more resistant set, one should say simply that it *changed* into a more resistant set. Since scientists for over a century have demonstrated that they are just as emotional in their convictions as nonscientists, let us choose our words wisely. Let science be unbiased in its semantics. We constantly need to refresh our understanding of what science is.

Duane H. Fickeisen, in his article "The Limits to Science," makes the following point:

> [S]cience is only one among many ways of studying the world. If we forget that, and expect science to give us an absolute answer to a problem, we invite misunderstanding.... As a body of knowledge, science is limited by our ability to observe and measure the world. It is also limited by the sheer volume of data available to us, and the uneven quality of the information we do have. ... Consequently we are forced to make inferences about the whole based on partial knowledge.

> To explain our observations, we develop theories. ... A proposed theory is rejected if it fails to explain the facts at hand. ... When a theory can no longer explain all the information, it is rejected in favour of one that better explains the facts.[4]

Within the limits of science, theories are explanations of scientific facts or laws; outside the limits of science, theories postulate unfalsifiable assumptions subject to debate. On the subject of phenotypes' origins, scientists are ignorant about the mechanisms involved. Some root them in creation and others in evolution. Unbiased science demands the examination of all possibilities irrespective of their philosophical implications.

In formulating the ground rules for scientific integrity, Nobel laureate Richard Feynman insists that "The idea is to try to give all the information to help others judge the value of your contribution, not just the information that leads to judgment in one particular direction or another."[5] What Feynman's observation indicates is that scientists are bound to consider both an evolution and a creation model, and that they should not exclude the possible roles of nonintelligent and intelligent forces in their investigation. Nothing in nature suggests that *nonintelligence* is more plausible than *intelligence*. It is naïve and wrong for scientists to think that the only way to discredit the likelihood of intelligent agencies in nature is to credit chance and nonintelligent processes. This makes a mockery of scientific methodology and flouts common sense.

The glory of science is to follow the evidence wherever it leads. To do otherwise is tantamount to a conflict of interest. Naturalism, materialism, creationism, evolutionism, and scientism are all belief systems, but science is a body of evidential and testable knowledge.

When science is based on empirical evidence (as opposed to circumstantial evidence), science becomes the only reliable way of understanding the material world. Unfortunately science is not the reliable way to understand the immaterial or spiritual world.

In evolutionary biology, while microevolution (bacteria-to-bacteria evolution), which is limited to the material world, is pure science because it is predictable, testable, and repeatable; macroevolution (bacteria-to-human evolution) involves both the material and immaterial realms, so just like special creation, macroevolution that results in transformations is a belief because the events are not testable, and repeatable. Accordingly, in the union between creation (a primary natural event) and evolution (a secondary natural event), macroevolution resulting in transformations is ruled out.

A blueprint for life presupposes a designer or designing instrumentality and a product. In world history, the Judeo-Christian God is the only one who has claimed credit publicly and civilly for having created the universe. Therefore in the creation-evolution unison, we will explore the role of God as the designer and the limited role of natural selection as a potential modifying mechanism.

NATURAL SELECTION IN THE CREATION-EVOLUTION UNISON

In the proper order, creation must precede selection; in other words, a selection event cannot take place without a prior creation event. Accordingly, a selector will always be subordinate to a creator. Scientists must therefore be modest and prudent in their choice of words in order to let science be science. Evolutionist Richard Dawkins, for instance, makes the outrageous claim that "[Genes] are in you and me; they created us, body and mind; and their preservation is the ultimate rationale for our existence."[6] Pierre Teilhard de Chardin posits that evolution "is a general condition to which all theories, all systems, all hypotheses must bow and which they must satisfy henceforward if they are to be thinkable and true. Evolution is a light illuminating all facts, a curve that all lines must follow."[7] Natural selection is not a deity. In the same spirit,

Darwin expected natural selection to be a marvelous designing instrumentality and proceeded without sufficient evidence to generate an imaginary tree of life.

Atheists Fodor and Piattelli-Palmarini point out the inconsistencies in Darwin's and neo-Darwinians' theories of evolution by natural selection:

> We don't claim to know *how* minds go about representing counterfactual events (or future or past events); or, for that matter, how they go about representing things that are right in front of their noses. Suffice to say that they can and do. It's therefore unsurprising that, when Gould and Lewontin wanted a good, firm, entirely intuitive example of the selected-for/free-rider distinction, they chose a case of *mental causation*, a case in which there *actually* is an 'intelligent designer'. So, too, did Darwin when he came to explain how natural selection works; the idea was that natural selection works just like breeding, *except that, in the case of natural selection, there isn't any breeder.*[8] (Emphasis theirs)

This is veridical evidence that in their theories evolutionists simply are replacing the role of an *intelligent designer* with the myth of *natural selection*. Their doing so ignores Feynman's ground rule for cultivating scientific integrity: "The first principle is that you must not fool yourself— and you are the easiest person to fool. So you have to be very careful about that. After you've not fooled yourself, it's easy not to fool other scientists. You just have to be honest in a conventional way after that."[9]

For natural selection to function, we need a raw material. Let us assume that the raw material is LUCA, the miraculous organism from which every living organism on earth supposedly descended. What does LUCA look like? Because no one knows, any guess that puts it close enough to a bacterium is reasonable. Its exact nature is not of interest. What instead engrosses attention is the alleged miracle that natural selection performs as the designing instrumentality. After millions of years of transformation, according to evolutionists, LUCA spawned human beings who were able to think, speak, acquire moral values, create wonderful things, and even tell stories about their origin. As Michael Denton points out, "[E]volution by natural selection is analogous to problem-solving without any intelligent guidance, without any intelligent input whatsoever."[10] With LUCA as the raw material and natural selection as the mindless instrumentality, scientists have plenty of unfalsifiable stories to tell our children. Adults of our present generation may or may not be influenced by Darwinists doctrines. However, in the wake of new atheism, youths are greatly influenced by it because it is fraudulently presented as a scientific fact. With the creationist worldview dismissed as a myth, the only option for students is to accept any theory of evolution as the truth and embrace atheism through science education.[11] When asked how the bacteria-to-human evolution would be implemented, many young people pause and invariably say "with time anything is possible." Anyone who chooses to face reality over fiction can always allude to a number of things that cannot happen given all the time there is. It was Nobel laureate George Wald on the subject "The Origin of Life and spontaneous generation" who wrote:

> One had only to accept the evidence of one's senses to know that life arises regularly from the nonliving: worms from mud, maggots from decaying meat, mice from refuse of various kinds. This is the view that came to be called spontaneous generation. ... I think a scientist has no choice but to approach the origin of life through spontaneous generation. ... One has only to contemplate the magnitude of this task to concede that the spontaneous generation of a living organism is impossible.

> Our everyday concept of what is impossible, possible, or certain derives from our experience: the number of trials that may be encompassed within the space of a human lifetime, or at most within recorded human history. In this colloquial, practical sense I concede the spontaneous origin of life to be "impossible." It is impossible as we judge events in the scale of human experience. The origin of a living organism is undoubtedly a stepwise phenomenon, each step with its own probability and its own conditions of trial. … The important point is that since the origin of life belongs in the category of at-least-once phenomena, time is on its side. However improbable we regard this event, or any of the steps which it involves, given enough time it will almost certainly happen at least once. … Time is in fact the hero of the plot. The time with which we have to deal is of the order of two billion years. What we regard as impossible on the basis of human experience is meaningless here. Given so much time, the "impossible" becomes possible, the possible probable, the probable virtually certain. One has only to wait: time itself performs the miracles [12]

Wald, because of his belief that time can perform miracles, initially ignored the scientific law of biogenesis that insists life comes from preexisting life. Wald's argument in favour of spontaneous generation is speculative and based on a very weak premise. What is fulfilling, however, is that Wald did not wait for time in order to discard his belief in spontaneous generation and embrace the fact that it is mind that composed the physical universe. Unfortunately, although there is no supporting evidence, modern evolutionists are not willing to discard the false notion of spontaneous generation, and are instead currently misleading students by positing that with time anything is possible.

But seriously, how would natural selection, an unconscious process, create consciousness and form intelligent beings? Genesis reveals that God formed the first human being from wet ground. No one knows what mechanisms were involved. The scientific establishment thus regards the creationist worldview as unscientific because the events are not testable and repeatable. In the evolutionist worldview, the role of God is replaced by natural selection as a mindless instrumentality. When we inquire about the mechanism involved in bacteria-to-human transformations, we get various answers. The honest answer is that "no one knows," which explains why scientists have been unable to reproduce the simplest laboratory evidence of a bacterium being transformed into a totally different organism. The dishonest answer is that "it would require a million years to implement any of these evolutionary transformations," such a long wait to produce just one new organism inhibit testability and reproducibility, hence, it is outside the purview of science. The common-sense answer is that, with LUCA as the raw material, it is impossible for natural selection as a blind and unconscious agent to manufacture eyes, develop ears, design noses, create mouths and install digestive systems, produce nerves, invent brains and encase them in skulls, and create genders for reproductive purposes without a prior knowledge of diversity.

Scientists who champion evolutionism have no genuine explanations of how natural selection would have produced humans from LUCA; the paradigm is based on faith, not science. Therefore, as the creationist worldview, the mechanisms in the evolutionist worldview are unknown; the events are not testable and repeatable. Accordingly both worldviews are unscientific! Why then is the scientific establishment promoting the evolutionist worldview as science? The only logical answer is that modern Darwinists are simply spreading the doctrine of new atheism under the umbrella of science.

Because the advocates of natural selection believe that it is an unintelligent instrumentality, the only logical conclusion is that it cannot be accountable as the central mechanism for biodiversity.

Accordingly, natural selection, like artificial selection, plays only a minor role as a modifying mechanism. This conclusion is consistent with the views of many who choose reality over fiction.

A CREATOR IN THE CREATION-EVOLUTION UNISON

In *The Language of God* Francis S. Collins, head of the International Human Genome Project, asserts:

> The human genome consists of all the DNA of our species, the hereditary code of life. This newly revealed text was 3 billion letters long, and written in a strange and cryptographic four-letter code. Printing these letters out in regular font size on normal bond paper and binding them all together would result in a tower the height of the Washington Monument.[13]

Amazed by all of this, President Bill Clinton in his speech heralding the venture's launching, said: "Today we are learning the language in which God created life. We are gaining ever more awe for the complexity, the beauty, and the wonder of God's most divine and sacred gift."[14] Some facts our brains may want to change but cannot. That we are spiritual beings in animal bodies is one of them. As Collins correctly posits, science's domain is to explore only nature as the material realm; it is incapable of exploring the spiritual domain.[15] God, however, operates in both domains. Collins therefore insists that we must find a way to embrace both realms.[16] Science tells us that we know comparatively little about the universe. "It turns out that roughly 70 percent of the universe is dark energy. Dark matter makes up about 25 percent. The rest—everything on Earth, everything ever observed with all of our instruments, all normal matter— adds up to less than 5 percent of the universe."[17] We thus are dealing with only a tiny fraction of the puzzle, which suggests that the mind behind this universe is beyond our imagination. I will again reiterate the following questions: If nonintelligence is behind the marvelous designs we observe, why should we need intelligence to investigate the evidence correctly? If chance is instrumental in shaping the universe, why does it obey natural laws that are antithetical to chance? If natural laws were generated by chance, they presumably would have vanished long ago; however, if they exist for a purpose, they are sustained to fulfill the purpose for which they were designed.

Natural processes are not sources of mental or intentional causation. Nature simply follows laws imposed on it by a lawgiver. Albert Einstein, for instance, did not believe in a personal God, but he believed in a God that created laws:

> I cannot prove to you that there is no personal God, but if I were to speak of him, I would be a liar. I do not believe in the God of theology who rewards good and punishes evil. My God created laws that take care of that. His universe is not ruled by wishful thinking but by immutable laws.[18]

Einstein is neither an atheist nor a conventional believer in God, so he speaks from the platform of pure science. In fact, Einstein insists:

> Everyone who is seriously engaged in the pursuit of science becomes convinced that the laws of nature manifest the existence of a spirit vastly superior to that of men, and one in the face of which we with our modest powers must feel humble.[19]

The holy Scriptures describe the Judeo-Christian God as a spirit who established the world by power, wisdom, and understanding and who operates by commandments or laws. According to the Scriptures, quite apart from natural laws there exist laws of the immaterial world unknown to human beings, who are the only creatures made in the image of God.

The mental causation that evolutionists wrongly attribute to natural selection derives from the immaterial or spiritual world that lies outside the domain of science. Nobel laureates Einstein, Wald, and Sir Ernst Boris Chain attest to the influence of this immaterial or spiritual world. Sir Isaac Newton, one of the greatest scientists who ever lived, wrote more volumes about God than science or mathematics[20] and credited all his discoveries to God's guidance.[21] Affirming Newton's intimate relationship with God, Gale E. Christianson writes:

> Unlike many thinkers today, he saw no conflict between science and religion and wrote that the world could not operate without God being present. ... Few things would have angered or dismayed Isaac Newton more than the claim by a later generation of thinkers that his discovery of mechanical laws established the framework of a universe in which God is no longer a vital, or even necessary, part.[22]

This puts to rest the modern misconception that great scientists do not believe in the existence of God. Any scientist who accurately reflects on the world would realize that explanations of the evidence based exclusively on materialism are inconsistent with reality and common sense. As long as the spiritual realm exists, God's role cannot be denied on scientific grounds. The question is, "Did God establish the world by a mindless mechanism (evolution) or by divine plan (creation)"? To answer this question we must first recognize three important points:

- Creation and evolution are both natural processes. Why is the scientific worldview only limited to promoting evolution as a natural process and not to both evolution and creation as natural processes? By restricting itself to evolution, the scientific community sets the stage to compete with religion rather than honor its moral obligation to search for nothing else but the truth. It will be dishonest to posit that evolution is the superior of the two. It is untrue to imply that there is no theory of creation.[23] The problem is that the theory of creation, just like the theory of evolution, does not meet the scientific requirements of testability and repeatability. The scientific establishment is only advocating the evolutionist worldview because it eliminates the need for a creator. Because evolution presupposes the existence of a raw material, it can only be a secondary process or event. For instance, in the laboratory scientists must first *create* an environment for the evolutionary event to occur. For the process of evolution by natural selection to operate, nature, if conscious and able, must first create the environment for the raw material to evolve. Even as a secondary process, evolution is thus subordinate to and dependent on creation.

- On the subject of the origins and relatedness of all species on earth, science can claim compelling circumstantial evidence but can never prove either creation by a designing agency or evolution by a designing instrumentality.
- The unequivocal proof of creation can be established only by the creator's formal and historical claim of responsibility before a live audience.

Two important schools of thought exist about God's role in the universe. One is affiliated with evolution as the primary and secondary mechanism, and the other with creation as a primary process and evolution as a secondary mechanism. Diversification through "descent with transformation" by natural selection will identify the "God of Darwinian evolution." Diversification through the creation of basic forms accompanied by "descent with modification" will identify the "God of Creation."

Collins is a strong advocate of the "God of Darwinian evolution."²⁴ Convinced that evolution might have been part of God's elegant plan for creating humankind, he cautions, "Freeing God from the burden of special acts of creation does not remove Him as the source of the things that make humanity special, and of the universe itself. It merely shows us something of how He operates."²⁵ Is special creation, one might ask, a burden to God?

The problem is that Collins' faith in Darwinian evolution, although grounded on the weak premise of genomes' similarity, is very strong. The fact that things are similar, however, does not necessarily mean that they must be related. Collins must also recognize that science cannot prove or empirically demonstrate Darwinian evolution by natural selection, just as it cannot prove or demonstrate God's special act of creation. In accepting Darwin's theory, Collins presumably dispensed with the burden of having to believe in God's special act of creation within six days.

To justify his belief in Darwinian evolution, Collins questions the literalness of Genesis 1 and 2.²⁶ Collins argues, "If a literal description was intended, why then are there two stories that do not entirely mesh with each other?"²⁷ After citing the opinions of other scholars, he concludes: "Despite twenty-five centuries of debate, it is fair to say that no human knows what the meaning of Genesis 1 and 2 was precisely intended to be."²⁸ An explanation is provided in the appendix of this book.

Genesis 1 details the order of creation. God personally confirms the six days of creation specified in Genesis 1 during the historic presentation of the Ten Commandments on ancient Mount Sinai. Moses described this event as an eyewitness in Exodus 19–20 and Deuteronomy 5. Collins himself believes in these commandments: "After twenty-eight years as a believer, the Moral Law still stands out for me as the strongest signpost to God. ...[G]od must be holy and righteous, since the Moral Law calls me in that direction."²⁹ He also believes strongly in the eyewitness account:

The concern about not accepting liberal interpretations of biblical texts is understandable. After all, there are clearly parts of the Bible that are written as eyewitness accounts of historical events, including much of the New Testament. For a believer, the events recorded in these sections ought to be taken as the writer intended—as descriptions of observed facts.[30]

So God, in claiming publicly to have created the universe in the number of days specified in Genesis 1, meets all of Collins' conditions for believability. In defending his belief in evolution, however, Collins posits the question "God as the Great Deceiver?"[31]

While it is proper to question stories in the Scriptures, bias intrudes when one presents similar stories that evolutionists present as scientific fact. Collins, for example, embraces the evolutionist story that dinosaurs dominated the earth about 230 million years ago and that their reign came to an end approximately 65 million years ago because they could not endure catastrophic climate changes resulting from a collision of planet earth with a large asteroid in the vicinity of Yucatan Peninsula. "That ancient asteroid collision," writes Collins, "is a tantalizing event. It may have been the only possible means by which the dinosaurs could have become extinct and mammals could have flourished. We probably wouldn't be here if that asteroid had not hit Mexico."[32] While sharing his passionate belief in evolutionary stories, Collins could have pointed to recent evidence that casts doubt on it. For instance, he might have mentioned recent evidence that dinosaurs ate grass,[33] which implies that dinosaurs may have coexisted with grass-eating mammals. There is also the 2005 discovery of soft tissue, blood vessels, and cells in the thighbone of a Tyrannosaurus fossil estimated to be 70 million years old.[34] This evidence challenges Collins' assertion that dinosaurs became extinct 65 million years ago. In accepting the evolutionists' story on dinosaurs, Collins disregards the story from creationists; he writes "One can even visit Creationist museums and theme parks that depict humans frolicking with dinosaurs, since the YEC (Young Earth Creationism) perspective does not accept the idea that dinosaurs became extinct long before humans appeared on the scene."[35] There are, however, credible revelations in the Bible that challenge the evolutionists' story on dinosaurs.[36]

The following questions that Collins poses in *The Language of God* are noteworthy. "Is not God the author of the laws of the universe? "Is He not the greatest scientist? The greatest physicist? The greatest biologist?"[37] The answer to all of these questions is a resounding yes, and that is precisely why God cannot be tailored to fit Darwin's theory of evolution by natural selection. Collins believes that God is unlimited by time and space[38] but by invoking mainly DNA similarity arguments to justify Darwin's bacteria-to-human evolution worldview, he limits God to the material realm and random chance. Collins understands that the spiritual realm belongs exclusively to God, but he fails to realize that contributions from the spiritual realm, which is impervious to science, are just as important as those from the material realm in order to understand the relatedness of organisms. All the relevant information must be on the table before science can draw definitive conclusions about our origins.

For some, circumstantial evidence is compelling enough to accept Darwin's theory of evolution by natural selection as truth, but for others circumstantial evidence is not compelling enough as it is subject to different philosophical interpretations. These minority skeptics prefer to wait for the first laboratory demonstration of molecule-to-human evolution. In the meantime, however, we must explore other means of procuring truth about our phenomenon world. A God of evolution is indistinguishable from random chance, hence, in biblical cosmology God uses the term "creation" to denote personal direct intervention and execution of every claim made in the holy Scriptures. Creation presupposes primary role while evolution presupposes secondary role. God's usage of the word "creation" is consistent throughout the Scriptures. Nowhere is the term "evolution" or a variant used. The closest to the concept of evolution is perhaps the command that each organism should produce after its own kind. By all indications, there is a limit to the kind of changes living things can undergo. This is a universal fact that evolutionists are reluctant to accept. We see these limits in the form of gaps in the fossil world and in the living world.

A God who establishes the universe by wisdom and takes personal interest in human beings, would claim ownership and let us know how and why the universe came into being, the reason and purpose of our existence and the rules and conditions for good living. A wise God would do this irrespective of whether we as creatures made in divine image would understand the mathematics and science of creation. This is exactly what the Judeo-Christian God did in the course of world history. God's claim for having created the universe is hard evidence for creation. John Rennie, chief editor of *Scientific American*, asked for evidence in which superintelligent agents publicly claim credit in order to override a purely evolutionist worldview.[39] My book *Farewell to Darwinian Evolution: Exposition of God's Creation Patent & Seal* was a detailed response to Rennie's demand for evidence. Below is a synopsis of the events that transpired.

In about 1445 BC, God scheduled three days in advance a meeting on Mount Sinai with the Israelites under the leadership of Moses. On the third day God, in no definite form or shape, descended to the summit. All assembled there stood a good distance from the mountain as God's voice thundered in declaring the Ten Commandments. God usually spoke in seclusion with Moses, but in claiming credit for creating the universe God spoke publicly to the crowd on their way to Canaan.

God's reasons were for the public to know the truth directly from the creator and lawgiver and also believe in Moses as the mediator between God and the Israelites in future matters. God's

Creation Sabbath Commandment (GCSC) is rendered as follows in the New Jerusalem Bible:

> Remember the Sabbath day, and keep it holy. For six days you shall labour and do all your work, but the seventh day is a Sabbath for Yahweh your God. You shall do no work that day, neither you nor your son nor your daughter, nor your servants, men or women, nor your animals nor the alien living with you. For in six days Yahweh made the heavens, earth and sea and all that these contain, but on the seventh day He rested; that is why Yahweh has blessed the Sabbath day and made it sacred (Exodus 20:8–11).

The GCSC is an abstract of God's patent and seal on creation. God is immaterial and hence uses an immaterial seal as an endorsement of his claim for having created the universe. The merit of an immaterial seal is noteworthy, for its parameter of time is everlasting, not requiring renewal as with conventional patents. In the light of the above, details of the GCSC taken from the New Jerusalem Bible (in bold print) appear below with explanatory notes related to a conventional patent (in brackets).

- [*WHAT?* There is a commandment to work six days but rest on the seventh day of the week.]

Remember the Sabbath day, and keep it holy [command to commemorate the Sabbath as the seal on creation of the universe, a ceremonial component]. **For six days you shall labour and do all your work, but the seventh day is a Sabbath for Yahweh** [name of God utilized in the capacity of sovereignty] **your God** [title of God]. **You shall do no work that day, neither you nor your son nor your daughter, nor your servants, men or women, nor your animals nor the alien living with you** [God's Creation Sabbath, unlike the exclusively Jewish sabbaths that point to redemption, is inclusive of all (see Isaiah 56), asserts equality and due respect for all living things, demands obedience and hence love for God, a moral component.].

- [*WHY?* Because God used six days to create the world and rested on the seventh day as evidence of completion of primary creation by direct intervention.]

For in six days Yahweh [name of God utilized in the capacity of a patentee] **made the heavens, earth and sea and all that these contain** [list of God's inventions, a creative component], **but on the seventh day He rested** [God did not rest from tiredness. He simply stopped: creating things (ex nihilo), rearranging the things created (such as separating the waters from dry land), and forming things from substances already created (such as making the sun and moon). God did not cease from the duties of sustaining, redeeming, or patenting the world.].

- [*HOW?* By power, understanding, and wisdom. Summary of events reported in Genesis 1 and 2.]

- [*SO WHAT?* The seventh day as God's seal on creation should be honored (Isaiah 58:13).]

That is why Yahweh [name of God utilized in the capacity of a patentor] **has blessed the Sabbath day and made it sacred** [The Sabbath is God's timeless seal on ownership of the world.].

[*SUPPORTING EVIDENCE*] For the period of forty years that the Israelites spent in the Arabian Desert, God identified the Sabbath day and provided evidence to parallel the six days of creation and seventh day of rest through the weekly schedule of supernatural delivery of manna (food in the form of coriander seed) supply to feed them. God supernaturally rained down the food supply six days a week with a double portion on the sixth day so that they can rest on the seventh or Sabbath day as commanded. The six days of gathering and processing the raw food supply paralleled God's six days of creation. The materials to create the physical world came from the immaterial or invisible world, and to hold this fact, God supplied the manna (food material) to feed people in the physical world from the immaterial realm.

To conform to conventional patent requirements, God wrote down the GCSC on tablets of stone. The wisdom of providing both oral and written testimonies in claiming credit for having created the universe should be evident. While the original inscription by the finger of God on stone tablets could be misplaced or destroyed by human beings (in fact, Moses out of annoyance over worship of the golden calf smashed the first set [see Deuteronomy 9 7: –29, 10:1–5]), the oral testimony could be passed on to future generation orally and/or in print.

God's claim for having created the universe is an historical fact. A commandment law is the highest level of authority that can be issued for a claim. Thus, in God's claiming credit for having created the universe, an event for which there were no human witnesses, a commandment law is not subject to debate because its authenticity, literalness, and timelessness are guaranteed. God therefore, from the very foundation of the world, provided a rebuttal to all opposing worldviews on origins. Evolutionists who continue to attribute the beginnings of life to chance and mindless processes are contravening God's patent rights of ownership.

God's claim for having created the world as a historical event is reported in Jewish history[40] and in *The Annals of the World*.[41]

Some have questioned, "What has God's claim before a crowd of ancient Israelites to do with the rest of the world?" Well, a claim concerning the creation of the world before a nation utilizes the recipient nation only as its domain of launching, and the world as its range of execution.

Scientists may not understand but cannot disprove or prove any of God's claims. Some scientists profess to believe in God but argue that the evidence they observe is not the product of the omnipotent and omniscient God depicted in scripture. For instance, Francisco J. Ayala, a world-famous biologist and leader in the religion-science field, argues:

> The design of organisms is often so dysfunctional, odd, or cruel that it possibly could be attributed to the gods of the ancient Greeks, Romans, and Egyptians, who fought with one another, made blunders, and were clumsy in their endeavours. But for a modern biologist who knows about the world of life, the design of organisms is not compatible with special action by the omniscient and omnipotent God of Judaism, Christianity, and Islam.[42]

What then is the role of the omniscient and omnipotent God of Judaism, Christianity, and Islam? The things God created were all good but human transgressions subjected them to corruption. As proof that the world was very good at the beginning, Adam lived 930 years, his son Seth lived 912 years and grandson Enosh lived 905 years (Genesis 5).

The gods of the ancient Greeks, Romans, and Egyptians did not publicly claim to have created the universe.

CREATION IN JUST SIX DAYS

Does it make sense for God to create as claimed in just six days? From the point of view of human being's ability, the answer is **no**, but from God's point of view, the answer is **yes**. Now from an analogical standpoint, one may also ask, "Does it make sense for human beings to complete and furnish a building in just a week, a month, or a year?" From the point of view of other organisms, like the earthworm, the answer is **no**, but from human being's point of view, the answer is **yes**.

In order to conform to the evolutionary predictions, some scholars and religious organizations try to explain away the six days of creation in Genesis 1 and Exodus 20:11, as representing millions of years. They are wrong for two important reasons. First, the Genesis account provides an unequivocal distinction between days and years (Genesis 1:14–16). Second, at ancient Mount Sinai, God speaking publicly commanded the observation of a seventh day Sabbath rest for living things (Exodus 20:8–11), and speaking privately with Moses commanded the observation of a seventh year sabbath rest for the land (Leviticus 25:1–4). While the seventh day Sabbath for living things is rooted to the creation of the world, the seventh year Sabbath for the land is not.

SUMMARY

It is common knowledge that species exist; however, due to limitations in both the material and immaterial realms, science cannot explain their origins and the mechanisms that produced them. It is complete nonsense to advocate any scientific theory that requires a million years to test its validity. Testability and reproducibility of events characterize what constitutes real science.

Creation is a primary natural process, whereas evolution is a secondary natural process. Change within time can be a consequence of either process. The creation–evolution unison is therefore an appropriate representation of the real world. By accepting microevolution as a scientific fact, creationists already profess this unison, but let it be so named to allow science to explore all possibilities in understanding our phenomenal world. Acknowledging the creation-evolution unison will dissolve the current designation of scientists as either creationists or evolutionists, and other variants (e.g., theistic and atheistic evolutionists) would soon disappear. The controversy within the scientific establishment is very bitter as I. L. Cohen explains:

> In a certain sense, the debate transcends the confrontation between evolutionists and creationists. We now have a debate within the scientific community itself; it is a confrontation between scientific objectivity and ingrained prejudice—between logic and emotion—between fact and fiction.[43]

The world has witnessed several cases of scientists arguing in courts of law in favour of either evolutionism or creationism. This robs science of its glory and integrity.

We can differentiate between evolution science (microevolution) and evolution dogma (macroevolution). All productive scientific research on biological evolution is confined to microevolution, which has beneficial applications in industry, medicine, and agriculture. Macroevolution is a myth because, among other things, it cannot address the immaterial dimension of living systems. Extrapolation from microevolution to macroevolution is scientifically impossible. What the creation-evolution unison does is to blend productive evolutionary science with the evidence of creation, including God's verbal and written claim for having created the universe. One must accept a claim that has not been and cannot now be disputed. Divine wisdom rests in the fact that God's claim of having created the world was issued under a set of moral commandments and comes with an immaterial seal, which suggests that it is everlasting; hence, there is no need for God to appear before another audience or nation to claim ownership. A commandment by the Almighty Creator is binding on all creatures regardless of whether they honor it or not. Just as no creature has a choice of whether to be born, no one has a choice in disputing God's authority as creator of the universe. Just as we cannot change the weather or climate, we cannot change what God has decreed; so the world is stuck with the weekly cycle of seven days that God commanded thousands of years ago. Nature encompasses (1) the material (visible) world plus the known laws and forces that govern change (this area falls within the scientific domain; the brain belongs here); and (2) the immaterial (invisible) world with its unknown set of laws and forces (this aspect falls outside the scientific domain; the mind belongs here). Just as the brain works with the mind, the known laws and forces in the material world similarly work in unison with the unknown laws and forces of the immaterial world. When scientists try to explain the universe only from the material point of view, their postulates usually defy common sense. Science alone is insufficient for a correct understanding of our universe.

Science is just one of several ways to understand the universe. The creation-evolution unison allows science to interact with other fields of knowledge such as religion to validate Einstein's assertion that "Science without religion is lame; religion without science is blind."[44] My proposal also recognizes a material-immaterial dualism, incorporates the limited role of natural selection, and above all validates the concept of a creator as axiomatic. The creation-evolution unison acknowledges God as both the author of religion and science. All this is evidence that the Judeo-Christian God is the infinite source of all natural laws both in the material and immaterial realms.

We conclude this chapter with the following remarkable quotation from Francis S. Collins:

> Will we turn our backs on science because it is perceived as a threat to God …? Alternatively, will we turn our backs on faith, concluding that science has rendered the spiritual life no longer necessary …?

Both of these choices are profoundly dangerous. Both deny truth. Both will diminish the nobility of humankind. Both will be devastating to our future. And both are unnecessary. The God of the Bible is also the God of the genome. He can be worshipped in the cathedral or in the laboratory. His creation is majestic, awesome, intricate, and beautiful—and it cannot be at war with itself. Only we imperfect humans can start such battles. And only we can end them.[45]

God is the embodiment of true religion and true science.

CONCLUSION

[R]eligion addresses the spiritual issues of life—those that cannot be quantified, examined under a microscope, or approved via the scientific method, for they are ultimately involved in a sense of wonderment about questions which cannot be answered by science.

The scientific enterprise, on the other hand, is stimulated by the same quest for knowledge and understanding but offers the practitioner the possibility of reaching his or her goal via the scientific method—seeing a problem, formulating a hypothesis, and being able to test that hypothesis until it is well-established as a theory or even fact.

[T]hen, religion and science form a linked dichotomy, in which the ultimate unifying factor is God at the base of the two branches.

Ultimately, the relationship between religion and science should be a complementary one, in which the pursuit of one is not exclusive to the other and in which indeed the pursuit of both can be synergistically more productive than concentrating on either alone. Only a person supremely self-confident and egocentric could conclude that one or the other of these branches was an end in itself, without being willing to consider the merits of the other parallel track.[1]

—Professor Thomas C. Emmel

> God is the author and embodiment of true religion and true science. In the natural realm and within the limits of science, creation is a primary process, and evolution is a secondary and subordinate process. In the modern scientific establishment, the creation–evolution controversy that is based on events outside the limits of science stereotypes members as creationists or evolutionists, but the creation–evolution unison that is based on events within the limits of science knits and blends members as scientists and creatures of God.
>
> —Michael Ebifegha

Because two organisms have similar material features, they should have a common ancestral progenitor. For Charles Darwin and his followers, this is sufficient reason to hypothesize bacteria-to-human evolution (macroevolution). However, both body (material) and mind (immaterial) characterize the development of living systems. When pictured from both of these perspectives, as opposed to only the material realm, would today's scientific community reach the same conclusion? Those who adhere to good science would say no because science does not understand the immaterial realm, but those who cling to materialism would say yes because their espousal of pseudoscience overrides scientific principles and laws. While science has limits, pseudoscience has none and hence plays to evolutionist Pierre Teilhard de Chardin's assertion that evolution is a movement whose orbit transcends the natural sciences and has invaded a myriad of other disciplines.[2]

This book looks beyond such simplistic and materialistic points of view. For instance, what would scientists deduce is the relationship between two organisms with (1) similar brains and minds, (2) dissimilar brains and minds, (3) similar brains but dissimilar minds, and (4) dissimilar brains but similar minds? Within the limits of real science, the answer is that the relationship is indeterminate. However, to Darwinists, there is no distinction because it makes no difference whether humans evolved from chimpanzees or chimpanzees from humanlike ancestors. Darwinists thus will give the same answer to all possible combinations since the preconceived conclusion is that they all share a common ancestor. This simple illustration fulfills the three attributes that Darwinists L. C. Birch and P. R. Ehrlick assign to evolutionism: (1) every conceivable observation can be fitted into it; (2) it is outside empirical science; and (3) no one can think of ways in which to test it.[3] Reaching the same conclusion for radically different events proves the inefficacy of evolution as a unifying theory in biology, unlike the atomic theory in chemistry and physics. Nobel laureate Ernst Chain thus perceives evolutionary arguments as "gross oversimplifications of an immensely complex and intricate mass of facts."[4]

Chain points out that evolutionists are more interested in morphological similarities than dissimilarities.[5] The fallacy of the similarity argument is evident in light of the "body-mind" dualism. If a morphological similarity between two organisms implies relationship, then a pronounced dissimilarity implies no relationship. If, for instance, the material and immaterial dissimilarities between chimpanzees and human beings outweigh their similarities, we anticipate an inconclusive relationship between them. If it turns out that the combined material and immaterial relationship between human beings and chimpanzees and that between human beings and birds or insects is not significantly different, this will contradict Darwin's theory that chimpanzees are our closest relatives. Because science has no knowledge about the immaterial realm, an authentic comparison of relationships between different kinds of organisms is impossible.

Genuine science relies on empirical evidence, repeatable observations, and testable explanations. If any of these conditions is not met, the theory is automatically outside the limits of science.

For instance, the origin of life or species is a singular event. It is not repeatable and cannot be tested. Accordingly, the Darwinian theory about the origin of species does not satisfy the requirements of real science. The very reasons that disqualify creation (a primary process) as a scientific worldview should now appropriately disqualify evolution (a secondary process) as the exclusive scientific worldview.

The current developments in evolutionary biology are not because of developments in the Darwinian bacteria-to-human paradigm of evolution by natural selection; it is the result of advances in the understanding of bacteria-to-bacteria paradigm of evolution.

Why, then, is the Darwinian evolution presented as genuine science while creationism or intelligent design is rejected? The truth is that Darwin's theory of bacteria-to-human evolution is not a fact of science but belief system that Darwinists perceive as the scientific alternative to the Genesis account on creation.

Even nature is not on the side of Darwinists. That life has progressed from simple to complex organization can only be confirmed unequivocally from a collection of fossils representing different organisms within the same geographic location. The fossil evidence at Burgess Shale in the Canadian Rockies and at the Chengjiang site in China, involving the abrupt and sudden appearance of a wide range of fully formed organisms with no *intermediary fossils, disqualifies* Darwin's theory of evolution from a common ancestor and hence invalidates his tree of life. The only evolutionary explanation why there are abrupt gaps in the fossil record is that the geological stratum is imperfect. This is a trivial reason. You do not have to be a scientist to offer lame excuses; science deals with evidence. Why then do we observe similar gaps in the living world? Is it also because the living world like the geological section is imperfect? The real reason is because Darwin's theory of evolution by natural selection is wrong and hence it does not fit the facts.

However, when scholars of a theistic orientation point out the inherent weaknesses of a Darwinistic paradigm, evolutionists become confrontational and insist on the separation of state and religion. Hopefully this attitude may gradually fade away with the recent surge of opposition from atheistic scholars. For instance, evolutionists Jerry Fodor and Massimo Piattelli-Palmarini distanced themselves from religious stereotyping in *What Darwin Got Wrong*, declaring that, although they are "outright, card-carrying, signed-up, dye-in-the-wool, no-holds-barred atheists," their reason for denouncing Darwinism is purely on scientific grounds.[6] In order to support their preconceived philosophical preference, evolutionists do two things. First, operating outside the limits of science, they engage in circular reasoning or utilize unfalsifiable assumptions to undermine the established principles and laws of science. Natural laws are timeless facts, but theories can change with new evidence. The law of biogenesis—life derives from preexisting life forms—prevails today, but then comes the Darwinist theory of abiogenesis that life derives from nonlife. Abiogenesis is not a demonstrable scientific law.

For life to arise spontaneously from matter is equivalent to winning a lottery without playing, which is only possible given the skewed logic of diehard Darwinists. Since no empirical evidence supports abiogenesis, the scientific establishment has created the Origin-of-Life Science Foundation and offered a one-million-dollar prize to scholar/s who can provide "a well-conceived, detailed hypothetical *mechanism* explaining how the rise of genetic instructions sufficient to give rise to life might have occurred in nature by natural processes."[7] A "hypothetical mechanism," however, cannot substitute for empirical evidence. Pseudoscience now makes its appearance, not hard evidence, to justify any preconceived materialistic dead-end. Abiogenesis is simply a scientism of the gaps that will only split rather than unite the scientific establishment.

The origin of the earth is unknown, so the origin of species cannot be related to it. Hence, arguments about the age of the earth or the ages of species and rocks that are based on circular reasoning are irrelevant to the creationism-evolutionism debate.

Second, evolutionists do not always follow the scientific evidence wherever it leads. The DNA molecule provides a glaring example of how evolutionists achieve their objectives by advancing conclusions that justify their philosophical preference but turn out to be antithetical to common sense and scientific inference. It is foolhardy for Darwinists to imagine, for instance, that intelligence is required for designing computer programs that utilize binary code but unnecessary for designing the sophisticated genetic program that uses quaternary code. This point confirms Chain's observation that scientists are prejudiced in their theories. Small wonder, then, that philosopher Antony Flew gave up atheism to endorse the concept of a sempiternal, immutable, immaterial, omnipotent, and omniscient being. The tree of life based on Darwin's theory of evolution by natural selection must be cut at its roots and the best way to accomplish this is what Flew utilized and atheists Jerry Fodor and Massimo Piattelli-Palmarini propose, "[T]o follow the arguments wherever they may lead, spreading such light as one can in the course of doing so."[8] There can be no computer program without a programmer; no blueprint without an architect; no photocopier without scientists and technologists and hence, no grand design without a designer. Science cannot eliminate the role of a creator.

Science is unable to prove the existence of either a common designer or a common ancestor; the choice between the two, consequently, is philosophical and not scientific. The notion of a designer, which creationists such as Isaac Newton and Albert Einstein acknowledged, is anathema to evolutionists such as atheists Richard Dawkins and Victor J. Stenger. Scientific data are always the same, but philosophical conclusions vary depending which scientists are dominant and/or steering the scientific community.

Regarding designing instrumentalities and agencies, there are two options: a dead source in the natural realm governed by chance and mindless forces; and a live source in the supernatural realm, a creator endowed with power, intelligence, and wisdom. Only a creator can justify the timeless scientific law of biogenesis and claim right of ownership of a property. The claim before a human audience must be consistent with conventional claims executed by human inventors. It must embrace the requirements of a conventional patent specifying the scope of the claim and a seal justifying rightful ownership. The Judeo-Christian God is the only being in world history who has fulfilled all of the above provisos. The claim of ownership was presented both orally and in print by God's finger on tablets of stone. The claim was structured in the form of a commandment law. God's claim to have created the world in six days, with cessation on the seventh day as evidence of completion (seal), is firm. The authenticity of this historical claim is irrefutable. The episodes of God's historical speech and documentation on stone tablets of having created the world were implemented at a particular point in world history. God, however, speaks timelessly and historically through the fossil records at the Burgess Shale and Chengjiang site. The truth in God's words is affirmed by the absence of intermediate states or transitional links in the living world.

Religion and science are currently at loggerheads by virtue of their proponents' alignment as creationists and evolutionists. For a unified truth, we must merge the historical evidence of God's claim to have created the world with the empirical truth of microevolution. This blending of religious truth and scientific fact is what this book terms the "creation-evolution unison." That God created the basic forms of living things with allowance for changes that do not exceed the boundaries of artificial breeding fully explain the abrupt gaps and diversity we observe in the fossil record and living world; changes from one kind to a different kind of organism are impossible so science is unable to establish even the simplest transformation. The creation-evolution unison embraces all truth—sacred, secular, and scientific.

The question of origins will remain a central issue as science advances and the agnostic-atheistic population soars. Philosophical preferences and circumstantial evidence may lead to preconceived conclusions, but, nonetheless, the truth is immutable. Creationism leads to theism; evolutionism leads to atheism; but the creation-evolution unison leads to correct understanding of our origins. The onus rests on every loyal and rational mind of what is proper and justifiable *in our world, where*: (1) an uncontested claim of ownership of property is honored without discrimination; (2) honesty and integrity at all levels of knowledge are timeless requirements; (3) science as a body of knowledge is limited; (4) religious and philosophical preferences are deemed personal; and (5) any form of potential child indoctrination via either religion or pseudoscience in the school curricula should be condemned.

APPENDIX

Genesis 2 highlights the similarity in material composition of living organisms and explores God's intentions for creation in order of importance. In Genesis 1, humans by divine order of creation came last; in Genesis 2, humans became first as the central focus of God's plan and essence for creation. In Genesis 1, the creation of birds was mentioned before wild animals but Genesis 2 is the reverse; hence there is some form of consistency. In Genesis 1, humans were commissioned to subdue the earth and have dominion over other living things. That mandate is reflected in Genesis 2. Scholars blend the two chapters without given much thought in an effort to justify their claims that the Scriptures should not be taken literally.

ACKNOWLEDGMENTS

My everlasting gratitude to God, the author of my mind and source of my strength.

My wife Margaret and daughters Marylyn, Mercy, and Michelle have been very supportive, and I profoundly express my love and gratitude to them.

Thanks are also due to Dr. Marc D. Baldwin and Robert Snyder of www.edit911.com, Rev. Dr. Ayyoubawaga B. Garfour, and Veronica Lee for her professional suggestions and support.

REFERENCES/NOTES

PREFACE

1. Stephen Hawking and Leonard Mlodinow, *The Grand Design* (New York: Bantam Books, 2010), 5.
2. Ernst Boris Chain, "Social Responsibility and the Scientist," *Perspective in Biology and Medicine in Modern Western Society* 14, no. 3 (1971): 353.
3. Stephen Jay Gould et al., "The Shape of Evolution: A Comparison of Real and Random Clades," *Paleobiology* 3, no. 1 (1977): 34–35.
4. James MacAllister, "Why Neo-Darwinism was the Biggest Mistake in the History of Science" The Royal Society's Evolution Meeting in London 2016. Posted: January 13, 2017, accessed July 31, 2020. https://evo2.org/royal-society-macallister/

INTRODUCTION

1. Andy McIntosh, Edgar Andrews, et.al., "Teaching of Origins in School: Letter to the Secretary of State for Education regarding the teaching of origins," *The Biblical Creation Society*, last modified April 24, 2003, accessed

May 23, 2010, http://www.biblicalcreation.co.uk/educational_issues/bcs116.html.
2. Michael Ebifegha, *The Darwinian Delusion: The Scientific Myth of Evolutionism* (Longwood, FL: Xulon Press, 2009), xxv.
3. Jerry Fodor and Massimo Piattelli-Palmarini, *What Darwin Got Wrong* (New York: Farrar, Straus, and Giroux, 2010), xx.
4. Ibid., 20.
5. Ebifegha, *The Darwinian Delusion*, 91–106.
6. National Academy of Sciences and Institute of Medicine, Science, *Evolution, and Creationism*, (Washington, DC: The National Academies Press, 2008), 12.
7. Ebifegha, *The Darwinian Delusion*, 209–71.
8. Emerson Thomas McMullen, "The Implications of the Cambrian Explosion for Evolution," accessed April 25, 2010, http://personal.georgiasouthern.edu/~etmcmull/CAM.htm.
9. Fodor and Piattelli-Palmarini, *What Darwin Got Wrong*, xiv.
10. W. Ford Doolittle, "Uprooting the Tree of Life," *Scientific American* 282, no. 2 (February 2000): 90–95.
11. Mary H. Schweitzer, "Blood from Stone," *Scientific American* 303, no. 6 (December 2010): 62–69.
12. Roger Highfield, "Large Hadron Collider: Thirteen Ways to Change the World," *Telegraph* (London), September 16, 2008, accessed September 25, 2010, http://www.telegraph.co.uk/science/largehadron-collider/3351899/Large-Hadron-Collider-thirteen-ways-to-change-theworld.html.
13. Large Hadron Collider, *Wikipedia*, accessed September 25, 2010, http://en.wikipedia.org/wiki/Large_Hadron_Collider.
14. Stephen Hawking and Leonard Mlodinow, *The Grand Design* (New York: Bantam Books, 2010), 180.

15. Fodor and Piattelli-Palmarini, *What Darwin Got Wrong*, xx.
16. Colin J. Humphreys, *The Miracles of Exodus* (New York: HarperCollins, 2003), 339–40.
17. Hawking and Mlodinow, *The Grand Design*, 123.
18. Ibid, 124.
19. John Rennie, "15 Answers to Creationist Nonsense," *Scientific American* 287, no. 1 (2002): 80.
20. F. Josephus, *The New Complete Works of Josephus*, trans. William Whiston, commentary by Paul L. Maier (Grand Rapids, MI: Kregel Publications, 1999), 118–21.
21. H. S. Lipson, "A Physicist Looks at Evolution," *Physics Bulletin* 31 (May 1980): 138.

CHAPTER 1

CONSTRAINTS IN SCIENCE

1. Deepak Chopra, "The God Delusion? Part 1," November 15, 2006, http://www.huffingtonpost.com/ deepak-chopra/the-god-delusion-part-1_b_34200.html. Accessed November 07, 2010.
2. Johan J. Bolhuis and Clive D. L. Wynne, "Can Evolution Explain How Minds Work?" *Nature* 458, no. 7240 (April 16, 2009): 832.
3. Kat McGowan, "Uncovered: How a Brain Creates a Mind," *Discover* (October 2010): 36.
4. Definitions of "materialism" on the Internet, accessed September 25, 2010, http://www.google.ca/search?hl=en&rlz=1T4ADBF_enCA291CA291&defl=en&q=de.
5. Definition of "dualism" on the Internet, accessed September 25, 2010, http://www.google.ca/ search?hl=en&rlz=1T4ADBF_enCA291CA291&defl=en&q=de.

6. Max Jammer, *Einstein and Religion: Physics and Theology* (Princeton, NJ: Princeton University Press, 1999), 93.
7. Special to the *New York Times*, "Obituary—Einstein Noted as an Iconoclast in Research, Politics, and Religion," *New York Times*, April 19, 1955, p. 25.
8. Richard Lewontin, "Billions and Billions of Demons," *New York Review of Books*, January 9, 1997, p. 31.
9. Michael Brooks, "Natural Born Believers: No Wonder Religion is Part of Human Nature— Our Brains are Primed for It," *New Scientist* (February 7–13, 2009): 31.
10. Ibid.
11. Ibid.
12. Randall Niles, "Philosophy: Dualism," accessed September 25, 2010, http://www.allaboutphilosophy.org/dualism.htm.
13. Brooks, "Natural Born Believers," 31.
14. Charles Darwin, *The Descent of Man, and Selection in Relation to Sex*, introduction by James Moore and Adrian Desmond (New York: Penguin Books, 2004), 150.
15. Ibid., 85–86.
16. Ibid., 85.
17. Ibid., 174.
18. Ibid., 85.
19. National Academy of Sciences and Institute of Medicine, Science, *Evolution, and Creationism*, (Washington, DC: The National Academies Press, 2008), 49.
20. Charles H. Smith, Introduction to "Alfred Russel Wallace: Evolution of an Evolutionist," accessed February 6, 2010, http://people.wku. edu/charles.smith/ wallace/chsarwin.htm.
21. Bolhuis and Wynne, "Can Evolution Explain How Minds Work?" 832–33.
22. Marc Hauser, "Origin of the Mind," *Scientific American* 301, no. 3 (September 2009): 44, 46.

23. David J. Buller, "Four Fallacies of Pop Evolutionary Psychology, *Scientific American* 300, no. 1 (January 2009): 74.
24. Ernst Boris Chain, "Social Responsibility and the Scientist," *Perspective in Biology and Medicine in Modern Western Society* 14, no. 3 (1971): 367–69.
25. Ken Meaney, "Hominid 'Ardi' Alters View of Evolution," *National Post*, October 2, 2009, p. A3.
26. National Academy of Sciences and Institute of Medicine, *Science, Evolution, and Creationism*, 33–35.
27. The Howard Hughes Medical Institute (HHMI), Species: Comparing Their Genome, 2001, http://www.actionbioscience.org/ genomic/hhmi.html, accessed November 30, 2010.
28. Melinda Wenner Moyer, "The Importance of Junk DNA," *Scientific American* 303, no. 6 (December 2010): 53.
29. *The Canadian Oxford Dictionary*, ed. Katherine Barbar (Toronto: Oxford University Press, 1998).
30. Hauser, "Origin of the Mind," 48.
31. Kathy Wren and Edward W. Lempinen, "Before 'Lucy,' There Was 'Ardi': First Major Analysis of One of Earliest Known Hominids Published in Science," *The American Association for the Advancement of Science* (AAAS), October 2009., accessed November 21, 2010, http://www.aaas.org/news/releases/2009/1001sp_ardi.shtml.
32. Emily Vincent, "Kent State University Professor C. Owen Lovejoy Helps Unveil Oldest Hominid Skeleton," public release date October 1, 2009, http://www. eurekalert.org/pub_releases/2009-10/ksuksu100109. php, accessed May 2, 2010.
33. National Academy of Sciences and Institute of Medicine, Science, *Evolution, and Creationism*, 32.
34. Darwin, *The Descent of Man, and Selection in Relation to Sex*, 154.

35. Ibid., 181.
36. Nina G. Jablonski, "The Naked Truth," *Scientific American* 302, no. 2 (February 2010): 42.
37. Ibid., 45.
38. Vincent, "Kent State University Professor C. Owen Lovejoy Helps Unveil Oldest Hominid Skeleton,"
39. Meaney, "Hominid 'Ardi' Alters View of Evolution," p. A3.
40. The Editorial Staff, *The Forerunner Forum*, "Is Evolution more Scientific than Creation?" http://www. forerunner. com/forerunner/ X0736_Is_Evolution_ Scienti.html, accessed November 22, 2010.
41. National Academy of Sciences and Institute of Medicine, Science, Evolution, and Creationism, 11.
42. Ann Gibbons, "A New Kind of Ancestor: Ardipithecus Unveiled," Tim D. White, et al., *"Ardipithecus ramidus* and the Paleobiology of Early Hominids," *Science* 326 (October 2, 2009): 43. 37, 60, 64.
43. Graham Lawton, "Uprooting Darwin's tree," *New Scientist*, (January 24–30, 2009): Cover page.
44. P. Z. Myers and Jerry Coyne, "New Scientist Flips the Bird at Scientists, Again," accessed January 20, 2010, http://richarddawkins. net/article/3667/New-Scientist-fl ips-the-bird-at-scientists-again/PZ-Myers-Jerry-Coyne.
45. Charles Darwin, *The Origin of Species* (London: Penguin Books, 1985), 455.
46. Kathy Wren and Edward W. Lempinen, AAAS, October 2009. http://www.aaas.org/news/releases/2009/1001sp_ardi.shtml., accessed May 2, 2010.
47. Deepak Chopra, "The Difference Between the Mind and the Brain," March 09, 2010, http://www.oprah. com/spirit/The-Difference-Between-the-Mind-and-theBrain/print/1, accessed November 12, 2010.

48. Chopra, "The Mind Outside the Brain (Part 4)," June 15, 2007, http://www.intentblog.com/archives/2007/06/the_mind_outsid_3.html, accessed November 12, 2010.
49. Thais Campos, "Where is the Mind? The Mind Exists Without the Brain," September, 2010, http://www.suite101.com/content/where-is-the-mind-the-mind-exists-without-the brain-a280509., accessed November 12, 2010.
50. Victor J. Zammit, "The Mind/Brain Debate in the Age of Science," http://www.victorzammit.com/articles/mindbrain.html., accessed November 12, 2010.
51. Deepak Chopra, "The God Delusion? Part 1," November 15, 2006, http://www.huffingtonpost.com/ deepak-chopra/the-god-delusion-part-1_b_34200.html, accessed November 07, 2010.

CHAPTER 2

CREATIONISM AND EVOLUTIONISM COMPARED

1. L. Harrison Matthews, introduction to *The Origin of Species*, by Charles Darwin (London: reprinted by J. M. Dent & Sons Ltd., 1971), x–xi.
2. The Editorial Staff, *The Forerunner Forum*, "Is Evolution More Scientific than Creation?" http://www.forrunner.com/forerunner/ X0736_Is_Evolution_ Scienti.html, accessed November 22, 2010.
3. Michael Ebifegha, *The Darwinian Delusion: The Scientific Myth of Evolutionism* (Longwood, FL: Xulon Press, 2009), xi–xii.
4. Michael Dowd, *Thank God for Evolution* (New York: Plume, 2009), 9.
5. Theodosius Dobzhansky, "Changing Man," Science 155, no. 3761 (1967): 409–10.

6. L. C. Birch and P. R. Ehrlick, "Evolutionary History and Population Biology," *Nature* 214, no. 5086 (April 22, 1967): 352.
7. Ebifegha, *The Darwinian Delusion*, 42.
8. Mario Seiglie, "The Evolution vs. Intelligent Design Debate—Interview with Dr. Jonathan Wells," *The Good News* 14, no. 6 (November– December 2009): 18. www.gnmagazine.org/issues/gn85/evolution-**intelligent-design**-debate.htm accessed November 24, 2010.
9. Ernst Mayr, *What Evolution Is* (New York: Basic Books, 2001), 163.
10. Pierre Teilhard de Chardin, *The Phenomenon of Man* (New York: Harper Perennial, 2002), 218–19.
11. Jonathan Wells, *The Politically Incorrect Guide to Darwinism and Intelligent Design* (Washington, DC: Regnery Publishing, 2006), 79–82.
12. Ibid., 82.
13. National Academy of *Sciences and Institute of Medicine, Science, Evolution, and Creationism,* (Washington, DC: The National Academies Press, 2008), xi.
14. Ibid.
15. Ebifegha, *The Darwinian Delusion*, 336.
16. L. Harrison Matthews, introduction to *The Origin of Species*, x–xi.
17. Richard Lewontin, "Billions and Billions of Demons," *New York Review of Books*, January 9, 1997, p. 31.
18. Jerry Fodor and Massimo Piattelli-Palmarini, *What Darwin Got Wrong* (New York: Farrar, Straus, and Giroux, 2010), xiii.
19. Michael Denton, *Evolution: A Theory in Crisis* (Bethesda, MD: Adler & Adler, 1986), 351.
20. Max Jammer, *Einstein and Religion: Physics and Theology* (Princeton, NJ: Princeton University Press, 1999), 48.

21. K. Ujvarosy, "Darwinism Delusion Exposed by Professor Emeritus of Biology," *American Chronicle*, January 9, 2007, accessed December 16, 2008, http:// www.americanchronicle.com/articles/18813.

CHAPTER 3

THE IRRELEVANCE OF THE EARTH'S AGE TO THE CREATIONIST/EVOLUTIONIST CONTROVERSY

1. Michael Ebifegha, *The Darwinian Delusion: The Scientific Myth of Evolutionism* (Longwood, FL: Xulon Press, 2009), 438.
2. Stephen Hawking and Leonard Mlodinow, *The Grand Design* (New York: Bantam Books, 2010), 124.
3. J. Perloff, *Tornado in a Junkyard* (Arlington, MA: Refuge Books, 1999), 146.
4. Gary E. Parker, *From Evolution to Creation: A Personal Testimony* (Waterloo, ON: Answers in Genesis, 2000), 10.
5. "Fossils and Rocks: Circular Reasoning," *CreationEvolution Encyclopedia*, accessed November 24, 2010. http://www.pathlights.com/ce_encyclopedia/Encyclopedia/12fos11.htm.
6. Hawking and Mlodinow, *The Grand Design*, 124.
7. David Shiga, "Earth may have had water from day one," *New Scientist* (November 05, 2010), http://www.newscientist.com/article/mg20827853.800-earth-mayhave-had-waterfrom-day-one.html, accessed November 07, 2010.

CHAPTER 4

THE ORIGIN OF LIFE AND SPECIES LIMITATION

1. Ricardo Alonso and Jack W. Szostak, "Origin of Life on Earth," *Scientific American* 301, no. 3 (September 2009): 56.

2. Michael Denton, *Evolution: A Theory in Crisis* (Bethesda, MD: Adler & Adler, 1986), 75.
3. Charles Darwin, *The Origin of Species by Means of Natural Selection of the Preservation of Favoured Races in the Struggle for Life* (New York: Signet Classic, 2003), 452.
4. "What Is Time? What Causes Time?", The Physics Blog, http:// www.timephysics.com., accessed November 24, 2010.
5. The Origin-of-Life Prize ®, About the Gene Emergence Project, accessed August 15, 2010, http://www. us.net/life/rul_abou.htm; The Origin-of-Life Prize ®, Description of the Prize, last modified July 2010, accessed August 15, 2010, http://www.us.net/life/ rul_desc.htm; The Origin-of-Life Prize ®, Prize Value, accessed August 15, 2010, http:// lifeorigin.org/rul_priz. htm; The Origin-of-Life Prize ®, Submissions, accessed August 15, 2010, http:// lifeorigin.org/rul_subm.htm.
6. National Academy of *Sciences and Institute of Medicine, Science, Evolution, and Creationism*, (Washington, DC: The National Academies Press, 2008), 22.
7. Scott C. Todd, "A View from Kansas on that Evolution Debate," *Nature* 401, no. 6752 (September 30, 1999): 423.
8. George Wald, "The Origin of Life," *Scientific American* 191, no. 2 (1954): 46.
9. George Wald, "Life and Mind in the Universe," in *Cosmos, Bios, Theos*, ed. Henry Margenau and Roy Abraham Varghese (La Salle, IL: Open Court, 1992), 218–19.
10. Mark Ridley *The Problems of Evolution*, (Oxford University Press, 1985), 7.
11. The Origin–of–Life Prize ®, Suggested texts, accessed November 12, 2010, http://www.us.net/life/rul_sugg. htm
12. Hubert P. Yockey, A "Calculation of the Probability of Spontaneous Biogenesis by Information Theory", *Journal Theoretical Biology*, (1977): 377.

13. Hubert P. Yockey, *Information Theory, Evolution, and the Origin of Life* (Cambridge: Cambridge University Press, 2005), 183.
14. Ibid., 186. Also see George Gaylord Simpson, "The Nonprevalence of Humanoids" *Science* 143 (1964): 769-775.
15. Hubert P. Yockey and Cynthia Yockey, "Information theory, evolution and the origin of life," February 20, 2009, http://www.hubertpyockey.com/hpyblog/, accessed November 12, 2010.
16. Jerry Fodor and Massimo Piattelli-Palmarini, *What Darwin Got Wrong* (New York: Farrar, Straus, and Giroux, 2010), xx.
17. National Academy of Sciences and Institute of Medicine, Science, *Evolution, and Creationism*, 10.
18. Hubert P. Yockey, *Information Theory, Evolution, and the Origin of Life* (Cambridge: Cambridge University Press, 2005), 188.

CHAPTER 5

THE NATURAL SELECTION LIMITATION

1. Gary Parker, *Creation: Facts of Life* (Green Forest, AR: Master Books, 2006), 87.
2. Jerry Fodor and Massimo Piattelli-Palmarini, *What Darwin Got Wrong* (New York: Farrar, Straus, and Giroux, 2010), 155.
3. Michael Ebifegha, *The Darwinian Delusion: The Scientific Myth of Evolutionism* (Longwood, FL: Xulon Press, 2009), 247.
4. Amazon.ca: Jerry Fodor, Piatelli-Palmarini: Books, accessed February 6, 2010, http://www.amazon.ca/What-Darwin-Wrong-Jerry-Fodor/dp/1846682193.

5. Fodor and Piattelli-Palmarini, *What Darwin Got Wrong*, 12.
6. Ibid.
7. Ibid., 122.
8. Ibid., 116.
9. Ibid., 10.
10. Richard Dawkins, *The God Delusion* (Boston: Houghton Mifflin, 2006), 79.
11. David M. Kingsley, "From Atoms to Traits," *Scientific American* 300, no. 1 (January 2009): 52.
12. Fodor and Piattelli-Palmarini, *What Darwin Got Wrong*, 120.
13. Ibid., 214.
14. Ernst Boris Chain, "Social Responsibility and the Scientist," *Perspective in Biology and Medicine in Modern Western Society* 14, no. 3 (1971): 357.
15. James MacAllister, "Why Neo-Darwinism was the Biggest Mistake in the History of Science" The Royal Society's Evolution Meeting in London 2016. Posted: January 13, 2017, accessed July 31, 2020. https://evo2. org/royal-society-macallister/
16. Andrew Mcintosh, In Six Days —Why 50 Scientists Choose to Believe in Creation, ed. John F. Ashton (Sydney: New Holland, 1999), 141–142.

CHAPTER 6

SIMILARITY/DISSIMILARITY LIMITATIONS

1. Truth in Science, "Comparative Genetics and Biochemistry," accessed October 9, 2010, http://www. truthinscience.org.uk/site/ content/view/143/65/. Board of Directors of Truth in Science include Stephen Hyde and Andy McIntosh.

2. Francis S. Collins, *The Language of God* (New York: Free Press, 2006), 6, 129.
3. Ernst Boris Chain, "Social Responsibility and the Scientist," *Perspective in Biology and Medicine in Modern Western Society* 14, no. 3 (1971): 357.
4. Kate Wong, "Jane of the Jungle," *Scientific American* 303, no. 6 (December 2010): 86.
5. Johan J. Bolhuis and Clive D. L. Wynne, "Can Evolution Explain How Minds Work?" *Nature* 458, no. 7240 (April 16, 2009): 832.
6. Marc Hauser, "Origin of the Mind," *Scientific American* 301, no. 3 (September 2009): 48.
7. Bolhuis and Wynne, "Can Evolution Explain How Minds Work?" 832.
8. Austin H. Clark, *The New Evolution Zoogenesis* (Baltimore: The Williams & Wilkins Company, 1930), 6-7.
9. Bolhuis and Wynne, "Can Evolution Explain How Minds Work?" 832.
10. Collins, *The Language Of God*, 63, 119, 123–24.
11. Truth in Science, "Comparative Genetics and Biochemistry."
12. Jill Bailey, ed., *The Way Nature Works* (New York: Macmillan, 1998), 96.
13. Collins, *The Language of God*, 133–34.
14. "Last universal ancestor," accessed October 1, 2010, http://en.wikipedia.org/wiki/Last_Universal_Common_Ancestor.
15. Collins, The *Language* of God, 125–26.
16. Truth in Science, "Comparative Genetics and Biochemistry."
17. W. Ford Doolittle, "Uprooting the Tree of Life," *Scientific American* 282, no. 2 (February 2000): 90–95.
18. Tina Hesman Saey, "Life Has Common Ancestral Source," *Science News* 177 (June 5, 2010): 12.
19. Ibid.

20. Ibid.
21. Mike Steel and David Penny, "Common ancestry put to the test" *Nature* 465 (May 13, 2010): 168.
22. Truth in Science, "Comparative Genetics and Biochemistry,"
23. Collins, *The Language Of God*, 6.
24. Ibid., 99.
25. Mike Steel and David Penny, "Common ancestry put to the test" *Nature* 465 (May 13, 2010): 169.

CHAPTER 7

THE NATURAL HISTORY LIMITATION

1. Jonathan Wells, *The Politically Incorrect Guide to Darwinism and Intelligent Design* (Washington, DC: Regnery Publishing, 2006), 16.
2. Mark Ridley, "Who Doubts Evolution?" *New Scientist* 90 (1981): 831.
3. E. J. H. Corner, "Evolution," in *Contemporary Botanical Thought*, ed. Anna M. MacLeod and L. S. Cobley (Edinburgh: Oliver and Boyd Ltd., 1961), 97.
4. "Natural history," *Wikipedia*, http://en.wikipedia.org/wiki/Natural_ history, accessed November 24, 2010.
5. Ibid.
6. Jerry Fodor and Massimo Piattelli-Palmarini, *What Darwin Got Wrong* (New York: Farrar, Straus, and Giroux, 2010), xx.
7. Henry Gee, *In Search of Deep Time Beyond the Fossil Record to a New History of Life* (New York: The Free Press, 1999), 7–9.
8. M. Lemonick, A. Dorfman, and D. Schrank, "Father of Us All?" *Time*, July 22, 2002, 38.
9. Charles Darwin, *The Origin of Species* (London: Penguin Books, 1985), 291.

10. Ibid., 315.
11. Ibid., 439.
12. Michael Denton, *Evolution: A Theory in Crisis* (Bethesda, MD: Adler & Adler, 1986), 57.
13. Ibid., 77.
14. Stephen Jay Gould, "This View of Life: Evolution's Erratic Pace," *Natural History* 86, no. 5 (May 1977): 14.
15. Stephen Jay Gould et al., "The Shape of Evolution: A Comparison of Real and Random Clades," *Paleobiology* 3, no. 1 (1977): 34–35.
16. Denton, *Evolution: A Theory in Crisis*, back cover.
17. Ibid., 160–62.
18. Madeleine J. Nash, "When Life Exploded," *Time*, December 4, 1995, 66–69. Jeffrey S. Levinton, "The Big Bang of Animal Evolution," *Scientific American* 267, no.5 (November 1992): 84–91. "The Cambrian Explosion—Biology's Big Bang?" http://www.allaboutscience.org/the-cambrian-explosion. htm, accessed November 28, 2010.
19. Denton, *Evolution: A Theory in Crisis*, 163.
20. Ibid., 176–77.
21. Ibid., 179.
22. Ibid.
23. Ibid., 180, 194–95.
24. Ibid., 87.
25. Richard Dawkins, *The Blind Watchmaker* (London:Penguin Books, 2006), 229.

CHAPTER 8

WRITING OFF DARWINISM

1. Michael Denton, *Evolution: A Theory in Crisis* (Bethesda, MD: Adler & Adler, 1986), 345.
2. I. L. Cohen, *Darwin Was Wrong—A Study in Probabilities* (Greenvale, NY: New Research Publications, 1985), 209.
3. Jerry Fodor and Massimo Piattelli-Palmarini, *What Darwin Got Wrong* (New York: Farrar, Straus, and Giroux, 2010), xx.
4. Ibid, p. 163.
5. Cohen, *Darwin Was Wrong*, 214–15.
6. Editorial, "Charles Darwin's Theory of Evolution Is Itself Evolving," *New Scientist* (January 24–30, 2009): 5.
7. Fodor and Piattelli-Palmarini, *What Darwin Got Wrong*, xiv.
8. Denton, *Evolution: A Theory in Crisis*, 358.
9. Pierre Teilhard de Chardin, *The Phenomenon of Man* (New York: Harper Perennial, 2002), 218–19.
10. Cohen, *Darwin Was Wrong*, 211.
11. Complete review, *What Darwin Got Wrong*, [an overview of the reviews and critical comments] http://www.complete-review.com/reviews/darwinc/fodorj.htm, accessed November 24, 2010.
12. Michael Ruse, "Darwin's Theory: An Exercise in Science," *New Scientist* 90 (June 25, 1981): 828.
13. Michael Ruse, "How Evolution Became a Religion: Creationist Correct?" *National Post*, May 13, 2000, national edition, p. B1.
14. Cohen, *Darwin Was Wrong*, 213–14.
15. Gary E. Parker, *From Evolution to Creation: A Personal Testimony* (Waterloo, ON: Answers in Genesis, 2000), 7. Dr. Gary Parker is an elected member of the national university scholastic honorary society Phi Beta Kappa,

recipient of two nationally competitive fellowship awards, and principal author of five programmed biology textbooks published by John Wiley and Sons.
16. Mary H. Schweitzer, "Blood from Stone," *Scientific American* 303, no. 6 (December 2010): 62–66.
17. Ibid., 68.
18. Ibid., 69.
19. Ibid.
20. Ibid.
21. Ibid., 67.
22. Ibid., 69.
23. Dolores R. Piperno and Hans-Dieter Sues, "Dinosaurs Dined on Grass," *Science* 310 (November 18, 2005): 1126.
24. Carl E. Baugh with Cliff ord A. Wilson, *Dinosaur: Scientific Evidence That Dinosaurs And Men Walked Together* (Orange, CA: Promise Publishing Co. 1991), 21-31; 53-60. Also see, Dinosaur and Human Footprints, Looking at Earth's Early History http://dinosaurc14ages.com/footprints.htm, accessed November 28, 2010.
25. Jerry Fodor and Massimo Piattelli-Palmarini, *What Darwin Got Wrong* (New York: Farrar, Straus, and Giroux, 2010), xiv, 20.
26. Denton, *Evolution: A Theory in Crisis*, 348.
27. Ibid., 348–49.
28. Ibid., 350.
29. Ibid., 351.
30. Tom Bethell, Evolution (Biology) –Philosophy. *American Spectator* 27, no. 7 (July 1994): 16. http://web.ebscohost.com/ehost/deliver y?vid=5&hid=12&sid=d3d1e1d967da-4616-aba4-c909219c2fb3, accessed April 29, 2008. Also see, Richard, The Framework of Evolution – part six, http://www.facebook.com/topic.php?

uid=107377179285980&topic=346 accessed November 30, 2010.
31. Richard Milton, *Shattering the Myths of Darwinism* (Rochester, VT: Park Street Press, 1997), x.
32. Denton, *Evolution: A Theory in Crisis*, 351.
33. Richard Dawkins et al., "Darwin was Right," http://richarddawkins.net/articles/3617, accessed November 30, 2010.
34. Charles Darwin, *The Origin of Species by Means of Natural Selection of the Preservation of Favoured Races in the Struggle for Life* (New York: Signet Classic, 2003), 452.
35. Ibid., 459.
36. Darwin, *The Origin of Species*, 438.

CHAPTER 9

THE MYTH OF THE GRAND DESIGN BY CHAOS

1. Stephen Hawking and Leonard Mlodinow, *The Grand Design* (New York: Bantam Books, 2010), 164–65.
2. Francis S. Collins, *The Language Of God* (New York: Free Press, 2006), 66–67.
3. Hawking and Mlodinow, *The Grand Design*, 5.
4. Stephen Hawking, *A Brief History of Time* (New York: Bantam Books, 1998), 191.
5. Hawking and Mlodinow, *The Grand Design*, 185.
6. Antony Flew with Roy Abraham Varghese, *There Is a God* (New York: HarperOne, 2007).
7. Richard Dawkins, *The God Delusion* (Boston: Houghton Mifflin, 2006).
8. Hawking and Mlodinow, *The Grand Design*, 172.
9. Ibid.
10. Hawking, *A Brief History of Time*, 190.

11. Ibid., 126.
12. Ibid., 146.
13. Hawking and Mlodinow, *The Grand Design*, 8.
14. Ibid., 153.
15. Ibid., 58–59, 83
16. Ibid., 153.
17. Stephen Hawking and Roger Penrose, *The Nature of Space and Time* (Princeton, NJ: Princeton University Press, 1996), 26; also S. W. Hawking, "The Nature of Space and Time," (online text) http:// arxiv.org/abs/ hep-th/9409195., accessed November 30, 2010.
18. Hawking and Mlodinow, *The Grand Design*, 8–9.
19. The Origin–of–Life Prize, Discussion, http://www.us.net/life/rul_ disc.htm, accessed November 30, 2010.
20. The Origin–of–Life Prize, Judging, http://www.us.net/life/rul_judg. htm, accessed November 30, 2010.
21. Hawking and Mlodinow, *The Grand Design*, 166.
22. Ibid., 8.
23. George Wald, "Life and Mind in the Universe," in *Cosmos, Bios, Theos*, ed. Henry Margenau and Roy Abraham Varghese (La Salle, IL: Open Court, 1992), 218. Nobel Prize for Physiology/Medicine (shared with Ragnar Granit and H. Keffer Hartline), 1967.
24. George Davis Snell, "I Do Not See How Science Can Shed Light on the Origins of Design," in *Cosmos, Bios, Theos*, ed. Henry Margenau and Roy Abraham Varghese (La Salle, IL: Open Court, 1992), 209. Nobel Prize for Physiology/Medicine (shared with Baruj Benacerraf and Jean Dausset), 1980.
25. *Webster's Universal Dictionary & Thesaurus* (New Lanark, Scotland: Geddes & Grosset, 2003), 280.
26. Hawking and Mlodinow, *The Grand Design*, 171.
27. Ibid., 161.

28. The Origin-of-Life Prize, Discussion, http://www.us.net/life/rul_ disc.htm, accessed November 30, 2010.
29. Hawking and Mlodinow, *The Grand Design*, 184.
30. George Wald, "Life and Mind in the Universe," in *Cosmos, Bios, Theos*, ed. Henry Margenau and Roy Abraham Varghese (La Salle, IL: Open Court, 1992), 218–19. Nobel Prize for Physiology/ Medicine (shared with Ragnar Granit and H. Keff er Hartline), 1967.
31. Ibid., 165.
32. Hawking and Mlodinow, *The Grand Design*, 124.
33. Ibid., 156.
34. Large Hadron Collider, *Wikipedia*, http://en.wikipedia.org/wiki/ Large_Hadron_Collider, accessed November 30, 2010.
35. George Musser, "The World's Biggest Particle Collider Might Uncover New Slices of Space," *Scientific American* 302, no. 6 (June 2010): 39.
36. Zeeya Merali, "Collider Gets Yet More Exotic 'To-Do' List" *Nature* 466 (July 22, 2010): 426.
37. Hawking and Mlodinow, *The Grand Design*, 134–35.
38. Craig Callender, "Is Time an Illusion?" *Scientific American* 302, no. 6 (June 2010): 59.
39. Christian Boehmer Anfinsen, "There Exists an Incomprehensible Power with Limitless Foresight and Knowledge," in *Cosmos, Bios, Theos*, ed. Henry Margenau and Roy Abraham Varghese (La Salle, IL: Open Court, 1992), 138. PhD in biochemistry, Harvard University. Nobel Prize for Chemistry (shared with Stanford Moore and William H. Stein), 1972.
40. Deepak Chopra, "The God Delusion? Part 7," December 04, 2006, http://www.huffingtonpost.com/ deepak-chopra/the-god-delusionpart-7_b_35513.html., accessed November 07, 2010.

CHAPTER 10

THE HISTORICAL RECORD OF GOD'S PATENT AND SEAL ON CREATION

1. Gary Parker, *Creation: Facts of Life* (Green Forest, AR: Master Books, 2006), 210.
2. Charles Hard Townes, "The Question of Origin Seems Unanswered If We Explore from a Scientific View Alone in *Cosmos, Bios, Theos*, ed. Henry Margenau and Roy Abraham Varghese (La Salle, IL: Open Court, 1992), 123. Professor of Physics, University of California. Nobel Prize in Physics 1964.
3. Robert Augros and George Stanciu, *The New Biology: Discovering the Wisdom in Nature* (Boston: New Science Library, 1987), 191.
4. Duane H. Fickeisen, "The Limit to Science," accessed March 20, 2010, http://www.context.org/ICLIB/IC32/Fickesn.htm.
5. Richard P. Feynman and R. Leighton, "Cargo Cult Science" in *Surely You're Joking, Mr. Feynman!: Adventures of a Curious Character* (New York: W.W. Norton, 1985), 341.
6. Richard Dawkins, *The Selfish Gene* (Oxford: Oxford University Press, 2006), 20.
7. P. Teilhard de Chardin, *The Phenomenon of Man* (New York: Harper Perennial, 2002), 218–19.
8. Jerry Fodor and Massimo Piattelli-Palmarini, *What Darwin Got Wrong* (New York: Farrar, Straus, and Giroux, 2010), 115.
9. Feynman and Leighton, "Cargo Cult Science," 341.
10. Michael Denton, *Evolution: A Theory in Crisis* (Bethesda, MD: Adler & Adler, 1986), 317.
11. Richard Dawkins, *The God Delusion* (Boston: Houghton Mifflin, 2006), 68; J. Allemang, "The Infinite Wisdom of

Richard Dawkins," *Globe and Mail* (Toronto), June 23, 2007, Focus F3.
12. George Wald, "The Origin of Life," *Scientific American* 191, no. 2 (1954): 45–48.
13. Francis S. Collins, *The Language of God* (New York: Free Press, 2006), 1–2.
14. Ibid., 2.
15. Ibid., 6.
16. Ibid.
17. Dark Energy, Dark Matter—NASAS cience, http://science.nasa.gov/astrophysics/focusareas/what-is-darkenergy, accessed November 30, 2010.
18. Max Jammer, *Einstein and Religion: Physics and Theology* (Princeton, NJ: Princeton University Press, 1999), 122–23.
19. Ibid., 93.
20. Gale E. Christianson, *Isaac Newton* (New York: Oxford University Press, 2005), 60.
21. Ann Lamont, 21 *Great Scientists Who Believed the Bible* (Acacia Ridge D.C., Queensland: Answers in Genesis, 1997), 47.
22. Gale E. Christianson, *Isaac Newton and the Scientific Revolution* (New York: Oxford University Press, 1996), 75.
23. Timothy Wallace, "A Theory of Creation: A response to the pretense that no creation theory exists," accessed November 17, 2010, http:// www.trueorigin.org/creatheory.asp
24. Francis S. Collins, *The Language Of God* (New York: Free Press, 2006), 163–64.
25. Ibid., 140–41, 146.
26. Ibid., 150.
27. Ibid., 151.
28. Ibid., 153.
29. Ibid., 218–19.
30. Ibid., 175. 31.

31. Ibid., 176.
32. Ibid., 95–96.
33. Dolores R. Piperno and Hans-Dieter Sues, "Dinosaurs Dined on Grass," *Science* 310 (November 18, 2005): 1126.
34. Mary H. Schweitzer, Jennifer L. Wittmeyer, John R. Horner, Jan K. Toporski, "Soft-Tissue Vessels and Cellular Preservation in Tyrannosaurus rex," *Science* 307 (March 25, 2005): 1952– 55.
35. Collins, *The Language of God*, 173.
36. Michael Ebifegha, Farewell to Darwinian Evolution: Exposition of God's Creation Patent & Seal (Longwood, FL: Xulon Press, 2007), 38–42.
37. Collins, *The Language of God*, 176.
38. Ibid., 7.
39. John Rennie, "15 Answers to Creationist Nonsense," *Scientific American* 287, no. 1 (2002): 80.
40. F. Josephus, *The New Complete Works of Josephus*, trans. William W. Whiston, commentary by Paul L. Maier, Grand Rapids, MI: Kregel Publications, 1999), 118–21.
41. James Ussher, *The Annals of the World* (Green Forest, AR: Master Books, 2003), 40–41.
42. Francisco Ayala, *Darwin and Intelligent Design* (Minneapolis: Fortress Press, 2006), 88– 89.
43. I. L. Cohen, *Darwin Was Wrong—A Study in Probabilities* (Greenvale, NY: New Research Publications, 1985), 7.
44. Max Jammer, *Einstein and Religion: Physics and Theology* (Princeton, NJ: Princeton University Press, 1999), 94.
45. Collins, *The Language of God*, 211.

CONCLUDING REMARKS

1. Thomas C. Emmel, "The Creative Process May Well Be What We Observe, Deduce, and Call Evolution," in

Cosmos, Bios, Theos, ed. Henry Margenau and Roy Abraham Varghese (La Salle, IL: Open Court, 1992), 167.
2. P. Teilhard de Chardin, *The Phenomenon of Man* (New York: Harper Perennial, 2002), 218–19.
3. L. C. Birch and P. R. Ehrlick, "Evolutionary History and Population Biology," *Nature* 214, no. 5086 (April 22, 1967): 352.
4. Ernst Boris Chain, "Social Responsibility and the Scientist," *Perspective in Biology and Medicine in Modern Western Society* 14, no. 3 (1971): 367–68.
5. Ibid., 368.
6. Jerry Fodor and Massimo Piattelli-Palmarini, *What Darwin Got Wrong* (New York: Farrar, Straus, and Giroux, 2010), xiii.
7. The Origin–of–Life Prize, Criteria for winning, accessed November 30, 2010, http://www.us.net/life/rul_crit.htm.
8. Fodor and Piattelli-Palmarini, *What Darwin Got Wrong*, xx.

INDEX

A

abiogenesis, 15, 63, 65, 81, 83, 171 *See also* origin of life and spontaneous generation.
age, *See also* time of dinosaurs, 122, 155–156
   of earth, 23, 70, 73
agency, 15, 23, 58, 74, 78, 84, 87, 125, 140, 153
Alonso, Ricardo, 76, 187
analogical reasoning, 48–52
Andrews, Edgar, 19, 179
Anfinsen, Christian Boehmer, 140, 198
angiosperms, 108
animals, intelligence of, 91–94
apes, relatedness to humans, 35, 38, 43–47
architectural age, 70–75,
Ardipithecus ramidus fossil "Ardi," 39, 43, 48, 50, 108
asteroid collision, and dinosaur extinction, 155
atheism, 24, 89, 131, 133, 147, 149, 172–174
Augros, Robert, 143, 199
Australopithecus, 39–40, 97
axioms, 83, 112
Ayala, Francisco, 161, 201

B

bacteria-to-bacteria evolution. *See* descent with modification
bacteria-to-human evolution. *See* descent with transformation
Bailey, Jill, 96 (In The Way Nature Works), 191
beliefs, versus theories, 46–48
Bethell, Tom, 125, 195
bias, in science, 88–89, 114–117, 143–145, 172
The Bible. See Scriptures
Big Bang, 129–130, 137–139, 193
biofilms, 121
biogenesis, 15, 63, 65, 81–83, 137, 140, 148, 171, 173, 188
Birch, L. C., 169, 186, 202
birds, 60, 92–94, 121–123, 169, 175
The Blind Watchmaker, 19, 110, 193
"Blood from Stone" (Schweitzer), 26, 118–121, 180, 195
Bloom, Paul, 33–35
blueprint, DNA as, 25, 96, 145, 172
Bolhuis, Johan J., 31, 36, 92–94, 181–182, 191
brain
   mind and, 31, 33, 41, 42, 50, 51
   size of, 39–41
Buller, David J., 37, 183
Burgess Shale, 25, 107, 170, 173

C

Callender, Craig, 139, 198
Cambrian fossil record, 20, 25, 65, 102, 108, 193,
Campos, Thais, 51, 185
"Can Evolution Explain How Minds Work?" (Bolhuis and Wynne) 36, 93, 181–182, 191
causation, 38, 76, 132, 146, 151, 152
CERN (European Organization of Nuclear Research), 137–138
Chain, Ernst Boris, 15, 38–39, 88, 91, 152, 169, 172, 179, 183, 190, 191, 202
chance. *See* random processes
change through time, 21
Chengjiang fossil site, 25, 107, 108, 170, 173
chimpanzees, brain size, 20, 45 See also apes, relatedness to humans, 37, 39, 43, 52, 91–94, 98, 108, 127, 169
Chopra, Deepak, 31, 50–52, 140, 181, 184–185, 198
Christ, on eternal life, 139
Christianson, Gale E., 152, 200
circular reasoning, 72, 85, 171–172
circumstantial evidence, 35, 39, 46, 68, 95–96, 110, 144, 156, 174
Clark, Austin H., 93–94, 191
Clinton, Bill, 150
coelacanth, 109
cognition. *See* mind
Cohen, I. L., 113–117, 163,–194
Collins, Francis S.
  DNA as language of God, 95,
  on science/religion domains, 100
  on genetic relatedness, 97
  on scientific limits, 90–91, 130
commonsense dualism, 34
computer systems analogy, 48–50
consciousness, 33, 41, 65–68, 135
Copernican theory, 123
Corner, E. J. H., 103, 192
cosmology, 80, 130, 137, 156
Coyne, Jerry, 126, 184
creation. *See also* descent with transformation
  versus creationism, 56–57
  domain of, 100.
  in Genesis, 73–74, 137, 154, 162, 170, 175
  Hawking on, 27–28, 131–134
  Mayan account of, 28
  as a primary process, 57, 95, 111, 153, 168
creation-evolution unison
  creator in, 150-161
  natural selection in, 145–150
  as representative of reality, 162–164, 174
  science in, 29
  scientific bias and, 143–145
creationism
  as belief system, 22, 65, 144
  investigation of, 27–28
  relatedness tests, 95–101
  worldview of, 137–140
creationists, 13, 15, 60, 68, 58, 163
creator figures, 150–161, 165
credibility, 14, 27, 46, 52

D

Darwin, Charles, 10, 35–37, 123, 127
"The Darwinian Delusion" (Davison), 68

The Darwinian Delusion: The Scientific Myth of Evolutionism (Ebifegha), 23, 62 –63, 86
Darwinian evolution
   earth's age and, 23, 73
   evidence cited for, 16, 39–48
   mind and, 35–39
   orthodoxy in, 26, 113–128
   scientific debate regarding, 163
   Teilhard de Chardin on, 60
   theories in, 38–39
   verifiability issues, 55, 73, 83
   as worldview, 57, 79 –83, 168
"Darwin was Right" (Dawkins, et al.), 126–127
Darwin Was Wrong (Cohen), 116
"Darwin was Wrong: Cutting Down the Tree of Life" (New Scientist), 48
Davison, John A., 68
Dawkins, Richard, 24, 87, 110, 126, 131, 145
Dennett, Daniel, 126
Denton, Michael
   on Darwin's general theory, 105
   on fossil evidence, 107
   on genetic programmes, 126
   on intermediate species, 109
   on natural selection, 147
   on missing links, 107
   on orthodoxy, in Darwinian evolution, 115, 124
   on randomness, 66
   on scientific validation, 76, 112
descent with modification. *See also* evolution
   defined, 21
   versus descent with transformation, 59, 63, 106, 125
   as domain of evolution, 144–145
   versus natural selection, 128
descent with transformation. *See also* creation
   defined, 21
   versus descent with modification, 59, 63, 106, 125
   as domain of creation, 144–145
designer, 25–6, 29, 50, 60, 63, 79, 84, 88–9, 96, 130, 140, 145–46, 172
dinosaurs, 104, 118–23, 155–56, 195
dissimilarity. *See* similarity/dissimilarity
distance, in measurement of speed, 77
diversity, within species, 24–5, 58–9, 86–9
divine plan, 152
DNA. *See also* genes; similarity/dissimilarity
   as blueprint for organisms, 25, 96, 172
   as evidence for evolution, 172
   as language, 95, 150
   life span of, 121–122
   relatedness of organisms and, 41, 96, 101
Dobzhansky, Theodosius, 57
Doolittle, W. Ford, 26, 180, 191
Dowd, Michael, 57
dualism
   commonsense, 34–35
   of material/immaterial realms, 27, 76–77, 164, 168–169
   versus materialism, 32–33

E

earth, age of, 70–75, 172
"Earth may have had water from day one" (Shiga), 73–74
Ebifegha, Michael, 70, 168, 180–187
Ehrlick, P. R., 169
Einstein, Albert, 32, 67, 80, 81, 92, 95, 133, 135, 140, 151, 152, 164, 172, 182, 186, 200, 201
Eldredge, Niles, 105
Emmel, Thomas C., 167
eternal life, 139
European Organization of Nuclear Research (CERN), 137–138
evidence. *See also* verifiability
   cited for Darwinian evolution, 16, 39–52, 112–128
   interpretation of, 104–105
   presentation versus evaluation, 130–131
evolution. *See also* descent with modification versus evolutionism, 57
   as material change, 42
   as natural process, 16, 57, 152
   as secondary process, 57, 95, 153
   as simple-to-complex process, 44 versus special creation, 102–103 verifiability of, 16, 112–113
evolutionary biology. *See* Darwinian evolution
Evolution: A Theory in Crisis (Denton)
   on fossil evidence, 104–110
   on natural selection, 147
   on orthodoxy, in Darwinian evolution, 115, 123–126
   on randomness, 66–67
   on verification, 16–17, 76–77
evolutionism, 22–25, 55–60, 65–68,
evolutionists, 13–15, 57–58, 169–173
experimental evidence, 15, 16, 19, 45, 50, 63, 66, 69, 76, 87, 103, 171.
   See also verifiability
extinct species, 48, 104, 109, 122, 155
eyewitness accounts, 9, 139, 154–155

F

falsifiability. See evidence; verifiability
Feynman, Richard, 144, 146, 199
Fickeisen, Duane H., 143, 199
Flew, Anthony, 131, 172, 196
Fodor, Jerry
   evolution as natural history, 27, 103, 113
   on natural selection, 24, 85–87, 146
   on orthodoxy, in Darwinian evolution, 9–10, 64, 114–115
   on rejection of Darwinism, 171
   on scientific evidence, 113
The Forerunner, 55, 184–185
fossils
   Cambrian, 20, 102
   as evidence for evolution, 39, 103–111, 170
   origins of, 23
   soft tissue preservation, 108–109, 118–123, 155
"Four Fallacies of Pop Evolutionary Psychology" (Buller), 37
"From Atoms to Traits" (Kingsley), 87, 190

From Evolution to Creation:
  A Personal Testimony
  (Parker), 117
functional characteristics of
  organisms, 103

G

GCSC (God's Creation Sabbath
  Commandment), 158–160
Gee, Henry, 103–104, 192
genes, 37, 41, 91, 98–99
Genesis, 25, 73–74, 130, 137, 148,
  154, 159, 161–62, 170, 175
geocentrism, 125
geological age, 70, 72, 75
God
  claim on creation, 28–29, 157
    58, 160–163, 173
  in creationism/evolutionism, 65
  as designer, 28–29, 63, 145
  evidence for existence of, 131–32
  in Genesis, 154–16
  Hawking on, 131–133
The God Delusion (Dawkins), 131
God's Creation Sabbath
  Commandment (GCSC),
  58–160
Goodall, Jane, 91
gorillas, brain size of, 43–4. *See
  also* apes, relatedness to humans
Gould, Stephen Jay, 15, 86–7, 105
The Grand Design (Hawking and
  Mlodinow), 27, 73, 129–135
gravity, 28, 127, 131–137

H

Hauser, Marc, 37, 41, 92, 182–3
Hawking, Stephen, 15, 26–8, 70, 73,
  129–140, 179–80, 196–98

Heliocentric theory, 47
historical events, 60
  Biblical records of, 28, 65, 138–
    139, 155–161
  not repeatable, 27
Homo erectus, 40
Homo habilis, 40
Homo sapiens, 40
horizontal gene transfer, 98
Horner, Jack, 118
humans
  genetic relatedness among, 97
  relatedness to apes, 40–48,
    91–92, 169
Humphreys, Colin J., 27, 181
hypotheses, 38, 60, 78, 104, 119

I

"I Do Not See How Science Can
  Shed Light on the Origins of
  Design" (Snell), 135, 197
immaterial realm
  limited knowability of, 140–141
  material realm, duality with, 15,
    20, 22, 35–6, 42, 94–5, 101,
    127, 135, 145, 162, 164, 169
  relatedness tests, 94–5, 103, 108
  scientific limits and, 16, 29,
    42, 52, 56, 73, 138, 152,
    164, 169
  similarities and, 25, 90–105, 169
  source of, 137
immaterial seal, 158, 163
information theory, 19, 81, 188–189
*Information Theory, Evolution, and
  the Origin of Life* (Yockey),
  81–82
*Information Theory and Molecular
  Biology* (Yockey), 81
integrity, in science, 23, 52, 63, 144

intelligence, 23, 49, 60, 65, 76, 137–38
intelligent design, 9, 59–61, 170, 186
intentional causation, 85, 88, 151
Israelites, 10, 28, 65, 157, 159, 161

J

Jablonski, Nina G., 45, 184
Jesus Christ, on eternal life, 139
junk DNA, 40

K

Kingsley, David M., 87, 190

L

language
  DNA as, 95, 150
  use of, by animals, 92
The Language of God (Collins)
  DNA as language of life, 95, 150
  on domains of science/religion, 100, 154–61, 164–165
  on genetic relatedness, 96–97 on scientific limits, 90–91, 129
Large Hadron Collider (LHC), 32–33, 136
last universal common ancestor. *See* LUCA (last universal common ancestor)
laws of nature. *See* natural laws
Lewontin, Richard, 33,.63, 87, 146
LHC (Large Hadron Collider), 26, 137, 180, 198
life, origins of. *See* origins, of life
The Limits to Science (Fickeisen), 143, 199
Lipson, H. S., 29, 181
Lovejoy, Owen C., 38, 43–45

LUCA (last universal common ancestor), 96–98, 146–49
Lucy fossil, 47, 97, 108

M

macroevolution. *See* descent with transformation
materialism, 14, 23, 32–3, 49, 65, 152
material realm
  evolution in, 42
  and immaterial realm, duality with, 20, 76–77, 127–128, 164–169
  origins of, 52
  relatedness tests in, 101
  science and, 20
  source of, 137
matrix age, 70-73
Matthews, L. Harrison, 55, 63, 185–86
Mayan creation myths, 28
Mayr, Ernst, 59, 186
McGowan, Kat, 31, 34, 181
Mcintosh, Andrew, 89, 190
McIntosh, Andy, 19, 179, 190
microevolution. *See* descent with modification
mind. *See also* immaterial realm
  human, 33–34, 37, 41–42, 49
  of superior being, 95
"The Mind/Brain Debate in the Age of Science" (Zammit), 51, 185
The Miracles of Exodus (Humphreys), 27
missing links, 20, 48, 103, 107, 110, 205
Mlodinow, Leonard, 15, 26–28, 70, 73, 129–140, 179–81, 187, 196–98, 207

modification, versus transformation, 21, 56, 59, 63, 106, 128, 153 . *See also* descent with modification
moral law, 154
Moses, 154, 157, 160, 162
M-theory, 131–135
multiple universes, 133–34, 137, 140
Myers, P. Z., 126, 184

N

"The Naked Truth" (Jablonski), 49
National Academy of Sciences and Institute of Medicine (NASIM), 36, 39, 44, 46–47, 61–62, 79, 83
natural history, limits of, 103--104
natural laws, 135, 137, 151, 164, 171
natural processes, 16, 20, 34, 49, 57, 60, 62, 73, 81, 88– 9, 151–52,
natural selection
    adaptability and, 58
    in creation-evolution unison, 145–150
    Davison on, 68–69
    versus creator, 172–174
    versus descent with modification, 127–128
    limits of, 35–36, 85–89
    as mindless process, 24, 98, 149
The New Evolution: Zoogenesis (Clark), 93–94, 191
New Scientist, 26, 48, 74, 114, 126, 182, 184, 187, 192, 194
Newton, Isaac, 152, 172, 200

O

objectivity, 31, 88, 163, 172. *See also* bias, in science

observation, ver*sus* experimental methods, 103–104
ontogeny, 69
organic materials. *See* soft tissues, fossil preservation of
"The Origin of Life and spontaneous generation" (Wald), 147–148
Origin-of-Life Science Foundation, 81, 134, 136–137, 171
The Origin of Species (Darwin), 104, 127
"Origin of the Mind" (Hauser), 37, 182–183, 191
Origins, 14, 27, 174, 179
    of design, 135, 197
    of life, 14–15, 36, 58, 79, 101
    of material realm, 52
    of species, 20, 22, 86, 103, 162

P

paleontology. *See* fossils
Parker, Gary, 71, 85, 117, 142, 187
parsimony, 122
peer-reviewed journals, 48, 79, 114
Petrovich, Olivera, 33
philosophy, versus science, 130
phlogiston, 52, 68, 124–125
phylogeny, 69
physical reality. *See* materialism; material realm
Piattelli-Palmarini, Massimo
    criticism of Darwinism, 171
    evolution as natural history, 27, 103, 113
    on natural selection, 24, 85–87, 146
    on orthodoxy, in Darwinian evolution, 9–10, 64, 114–115
    on scientific evidence, 113

The Politically Incorrect Guide to Darwinism and Intelligent Design (Wells), 61
primary, versus secondary processes, 57
primeval/prebiotic soup, 82
proof of evolution, in science, 55, 68–9
proteins, 56, 97–100, 119–121
pseudoscience, 14, 37, 56, 168, 171
Ptolemaic theory, 123–124
punctuated equilibrium, 15, 105

Q

quantum mechanics, 135, 140
quantum theory, 133

R

radiometric dating, 71–72
random processes
    Denton on, 125–126
    in evolutionism, 67–68
    vs. intelligence, 49, 172–173
    natural selection as, 24–5, 98
    Origin-of-Life Science Foundation on, 136
relatedness tests, 31, 41, 95. *See also* similarity/dissimilarity
religion. *See also* immaterial realm
    criticism of, by Darwinians, 125
    domain of inquiry for, 100, 154–161, 163–165
    dualism and, 32–33
    relationship with science, 164
    schools and, 174
Rennie, John, 28, 157, 181, 201
repeatability, in scientific verification, 13, 52, 62, 153
reproduction, sexual, 67

Rhipidistia, 109
Ridley, Mark, 81, 102, 188, 192
Ruse, Michael, 116, 194

S

Sabbath day, 158–160
School curricula, 56, 174
Schweitzer, Mary H., 32, 117–121
science. *See also* material realm; scientific limits
    as one form of knowledge, 33, 164
    bias in, 88, 114–117, 143–144, 172
    domain of inquiry for, 99–100, 144–145, 154–165
    integrity in, 52, 63, 81, 114, 117, 126, 144, 146, 163
    materiality and, 14, 20, 31, 33
    versus philosophy, 15, 130
    relationship with religion, 164
    revolutions in, 123–126
    schools and, 174
Science, Evolution, and Creationism (NASIM), 36, 39, 44, 46, 47, 61, 62, 79, 83
Scientific American, 26, 28, 45, 91, 118, 157, 181–84, 187, 188, 190, 191, 193, 195, 198, 200, 201
scientific limits
    areas of inquiry, 13–14, 90–91
    evidence and, 129–130
    Fickeisen on, 143, 199
    immaterial realm beyond scientific inquiry, 28–29, 37–38, 97–98, 100–101
    known universe and, 150–151
    origin of life not replicable, 14–15, 22, 84
Scriptures

on creation, 73–74
earth created for habitation, 137
eternal life, 139
Genesis, 25, 73–74, 130, 137, 148, 154, 159, 161–62, 170, 175
God as creator, 151–152
on human ancestors, 97
on human mind, 34
on similarities, 60, 91
secondary, vs. primary processes, 57
sexual reproduction, 67
Shiga, David, 74, 187
similarity/ dissimilarity, 25, 39, 90, 91, 94–97, 100, 101, 154, 156, 169, 175
Simpson, George Gaylord, 82, 189
six days of creation, 73, 154, 160–2
Snell, George Davis, 135, 197
soft tissues, fossil preservation of, 109, 118–123, 155
special creation, 55, 73, 80, 102, 103, 145, 154
speed, determination of, 77
spiritual realm, 33, 100, 135, 152, 156, *See also* immaterial realm
spontaneous creation, 28, 131–132
spontaneous generation, 15, 38, 65, 80, 89, 137, 140, 147, 148, *See also* abiogenesis
Stanciu, George, 143, 199
structural age, 70–72
subjectivity. *See* bias, in science
Szostak, Jack W., 76, 187

T

Teilhard de Chardin, Pierre, 60, 115, 145, 168, 186, 194, 199, 202
Ten Commandments, 154, 157
testability. *See* verifiability

Thank God for Evolution (Dowd), 57, 185
Theobald, Douglas, 99–101
theoretical assumptions, 138
theories in science, 36, 47, 52, 68, 73, 83, 106, 123–125
theory of everything, 131, 135, 140
There is a God (Flew), 131; 172, 196
time, 73, 77, 139, See also age
Todd, Scott, 79, 188
Townes, Charles H., 142, 199
transformation, versus modification, 59, 63. *See also* descent with transformation
transitional stages. *See* missing links
tree of life analogy, 42, 98, 114, 126, 172
Truth in Science Organization, 90, 95–99

U

Uncovered: How a Brain Creates a Mind" (McGowan), 31, 34
uniformitarianism, 81

V

verifiability. See also evidence
criteria for, 13, 103–104, 134–36
evolutionary theory and, 46–48, 55, 83
experimental evidence and, 19, 68–69, 76, 103–104
of hypotheses, 78
proof and, 55, 67–68
repeatability and, 16, 55, 69, 76, 108, 145, 149
in science, 14–17
vertical gene transfer, 98
Vincent, Emily, 43, 183–184

W

Wald, George, 80–81, 95, 135, 137, 147–8, 152, 188, 197–8
Wallace, Alfred Russell, 36, 129, 182
water, earth's age and, 73–75
The Way Nature Works (Bailey), 96
Wells, Jonathan, 59, 61, 102, 186, 192, 209
What Darwin Got Wrong (Fodor and Piattelli-Palmarini)
    authors' position on criticism of evolution, 171
    evolution as natural history, 103
    on natural selection, 24, 85, 87, 146
    on orthodoxy, in Darwinian evolution, 10, 115
    on scientific evidence, 113
White, Tim, 50, 184
Wong, Kate, 91, 191
Wynne, Clive D. L 31, 36, 92–93, 181–182, 191

Y

Yockey, Cynthi, 82
Yockey, Hu, 81–84, 188–189, 207
Young Earth Creationism (YEC), 156

Z

Zammit, Victor J., 51, 185, 208

www.ingramcontent.com/pod-product-compliance
Lightning Source LLC
LaVergne TN
LVHW021711060526
838200LV00050B/2603